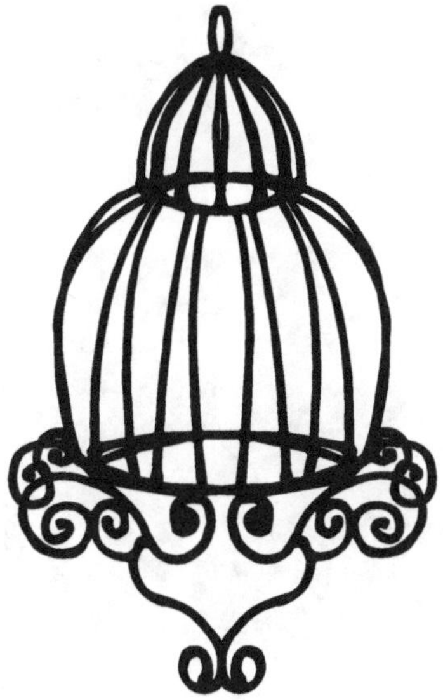

This book belongs to:

_____

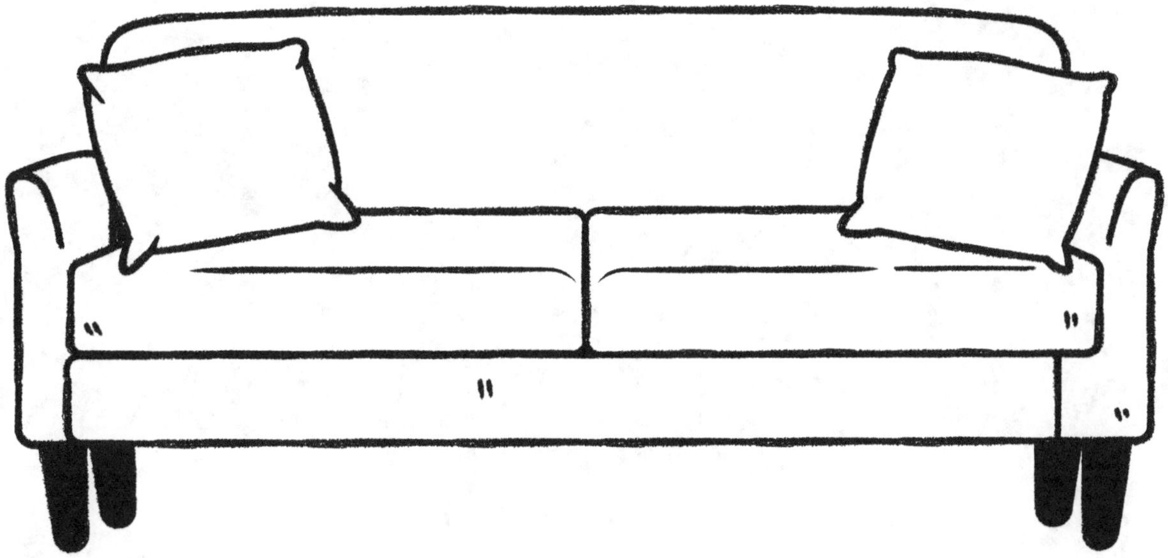

Home, the spot of earth supremely blest,
a dearer, sweeter spot than all the rest.

Robert Montgomery

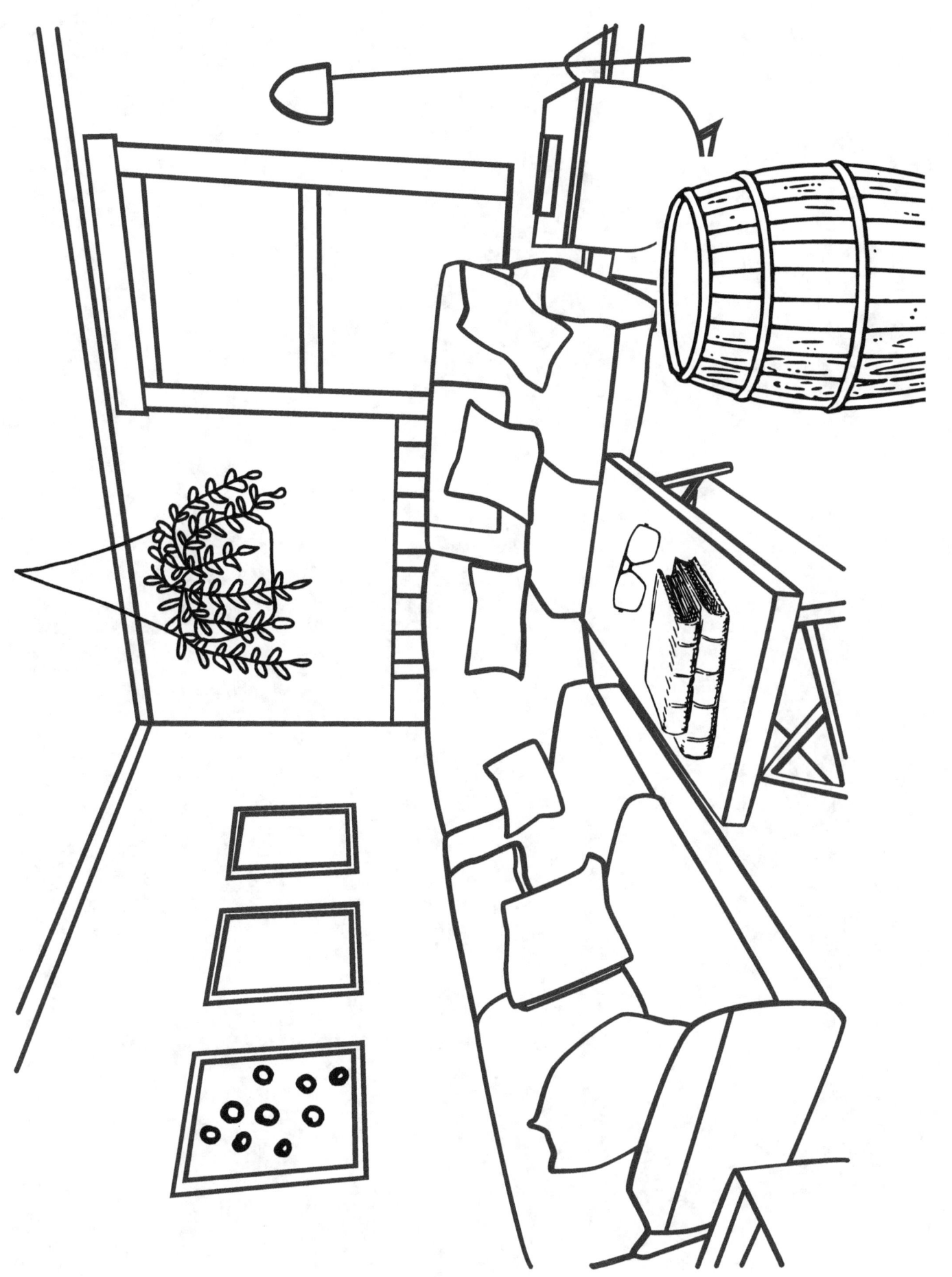

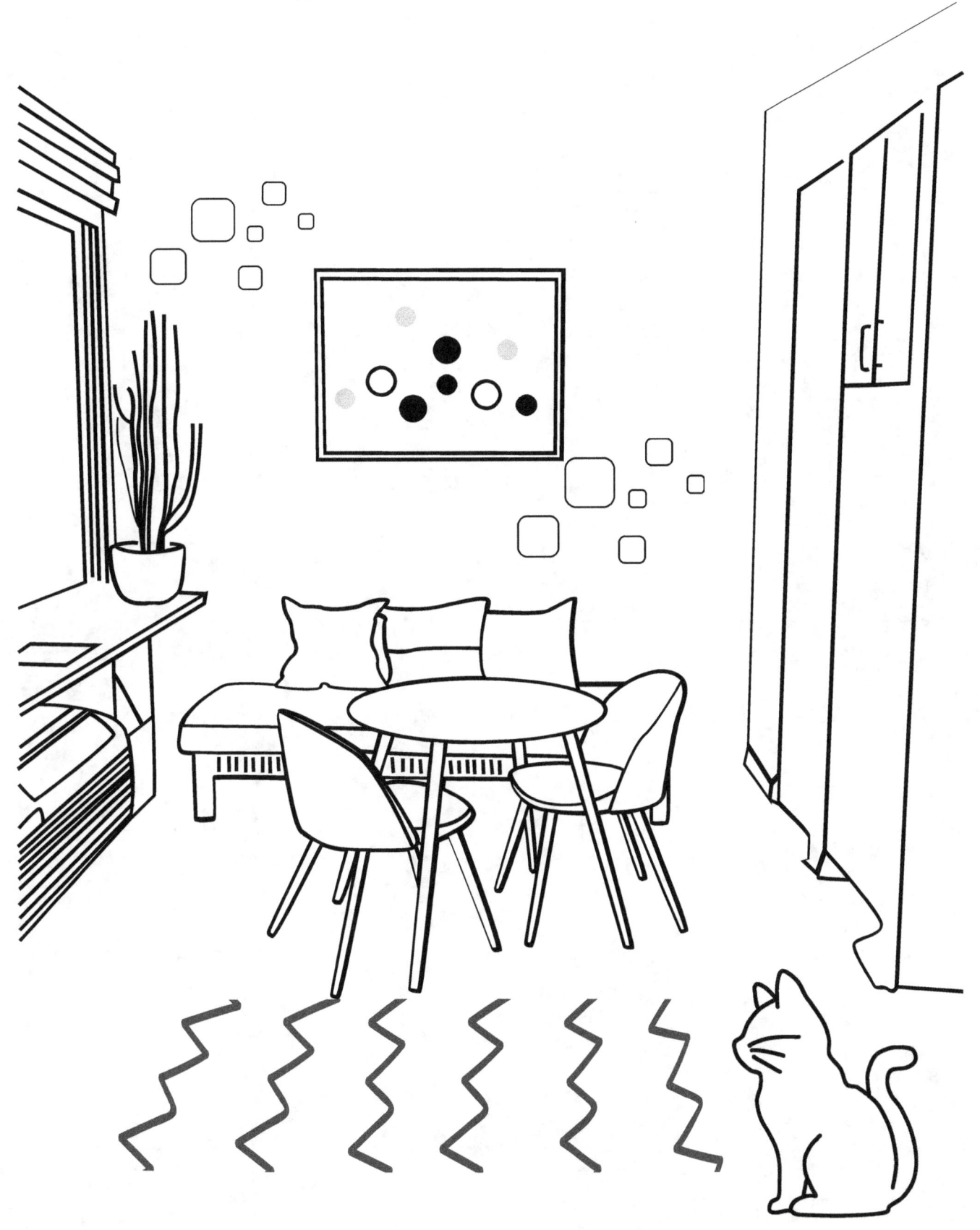

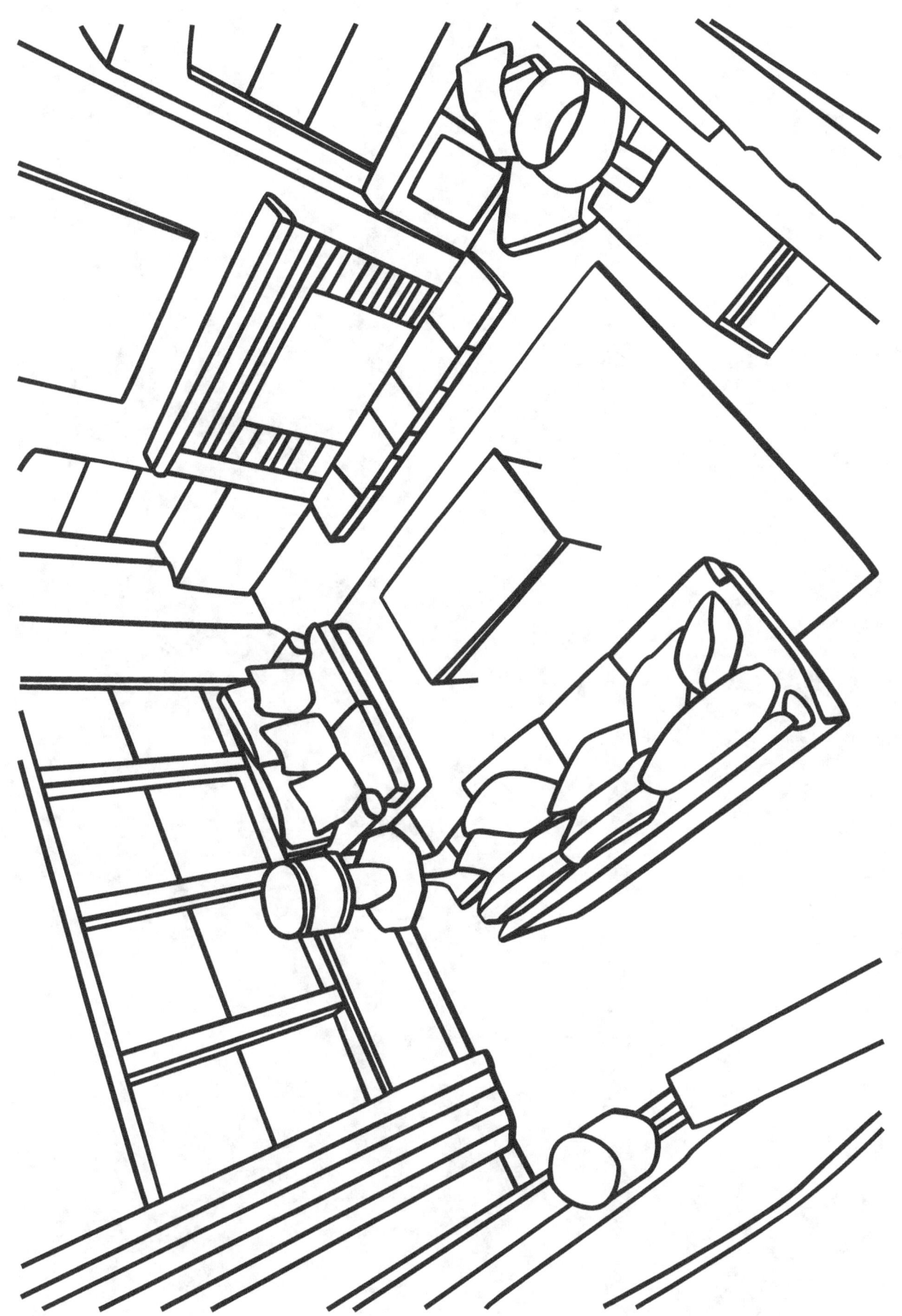

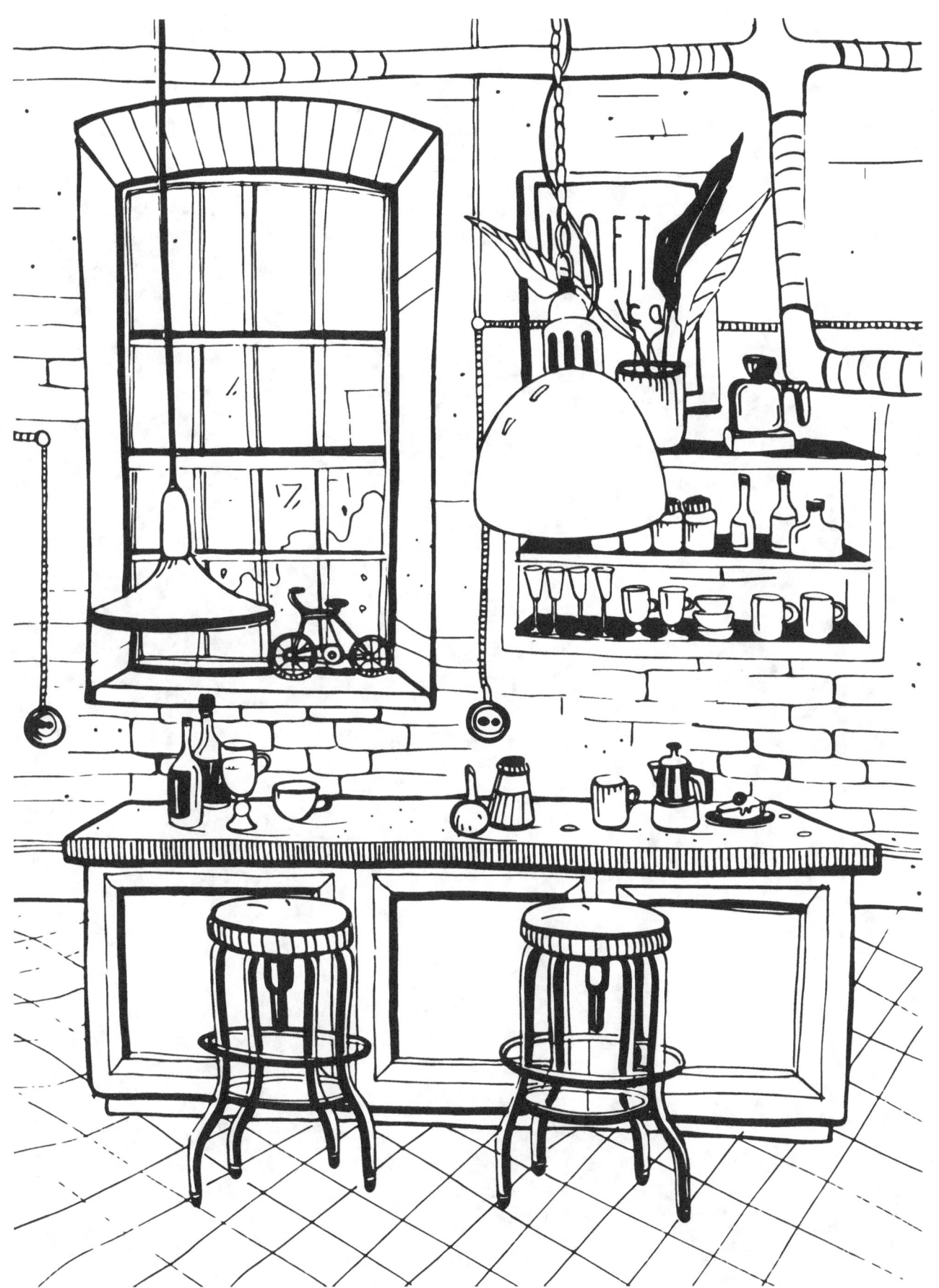

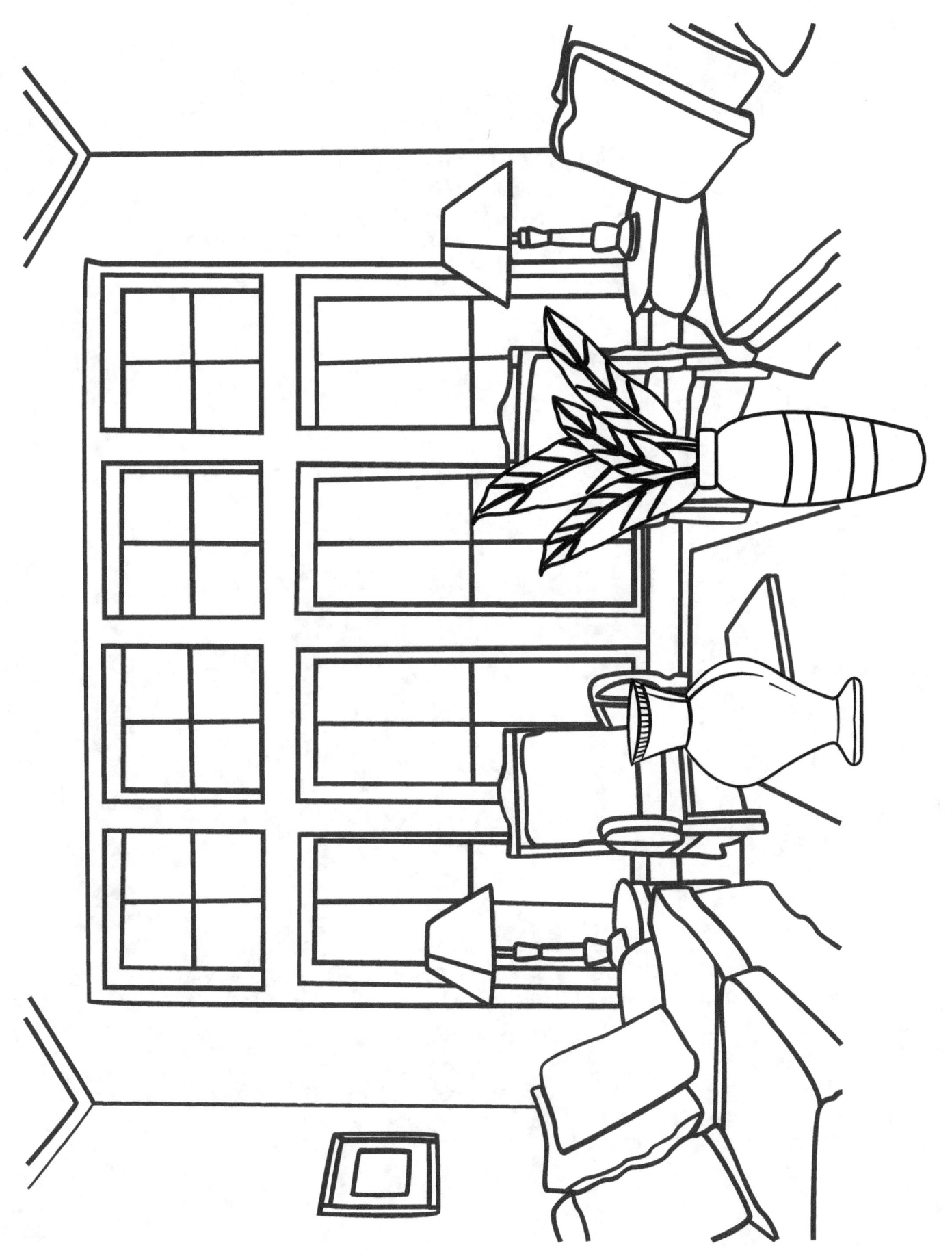

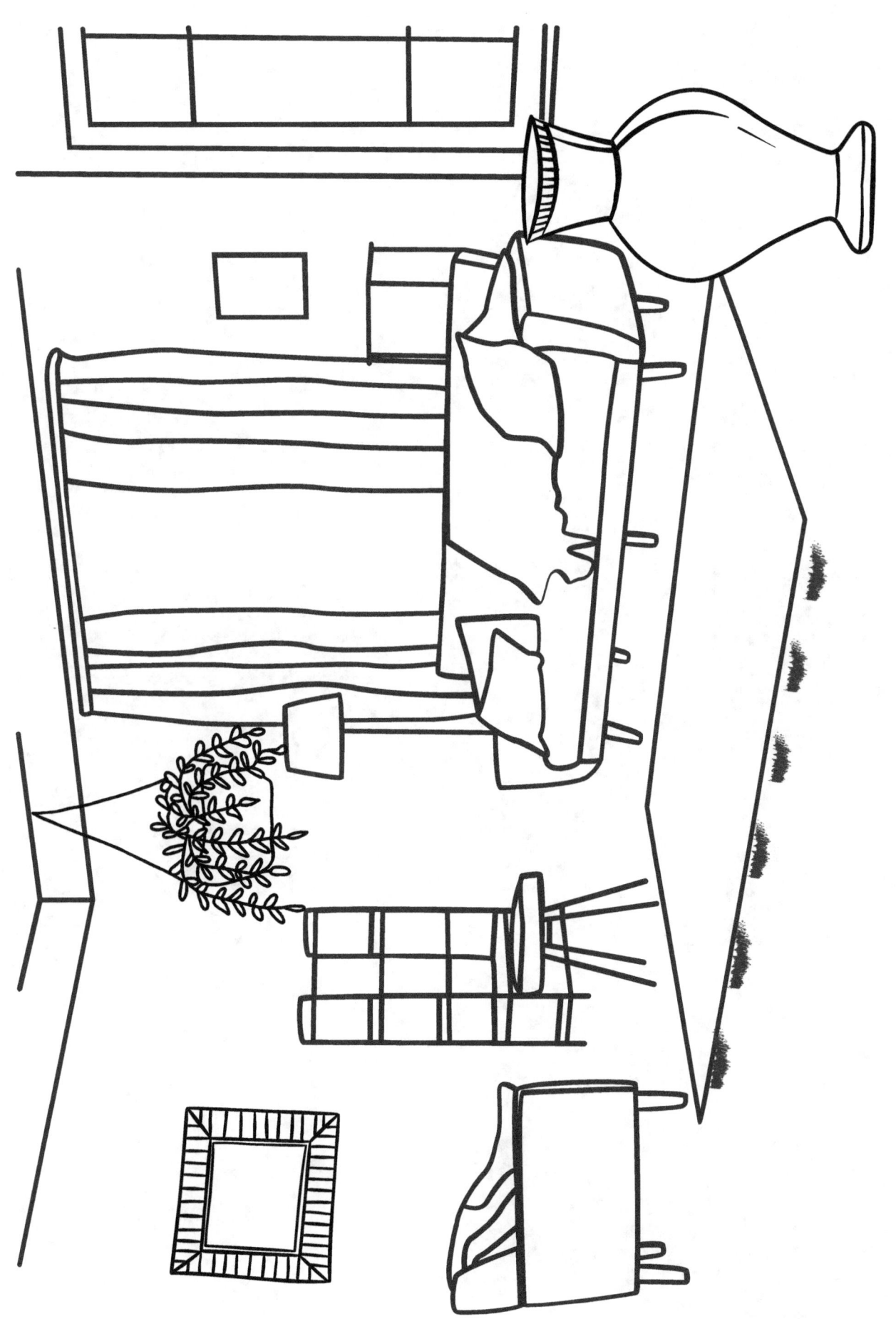

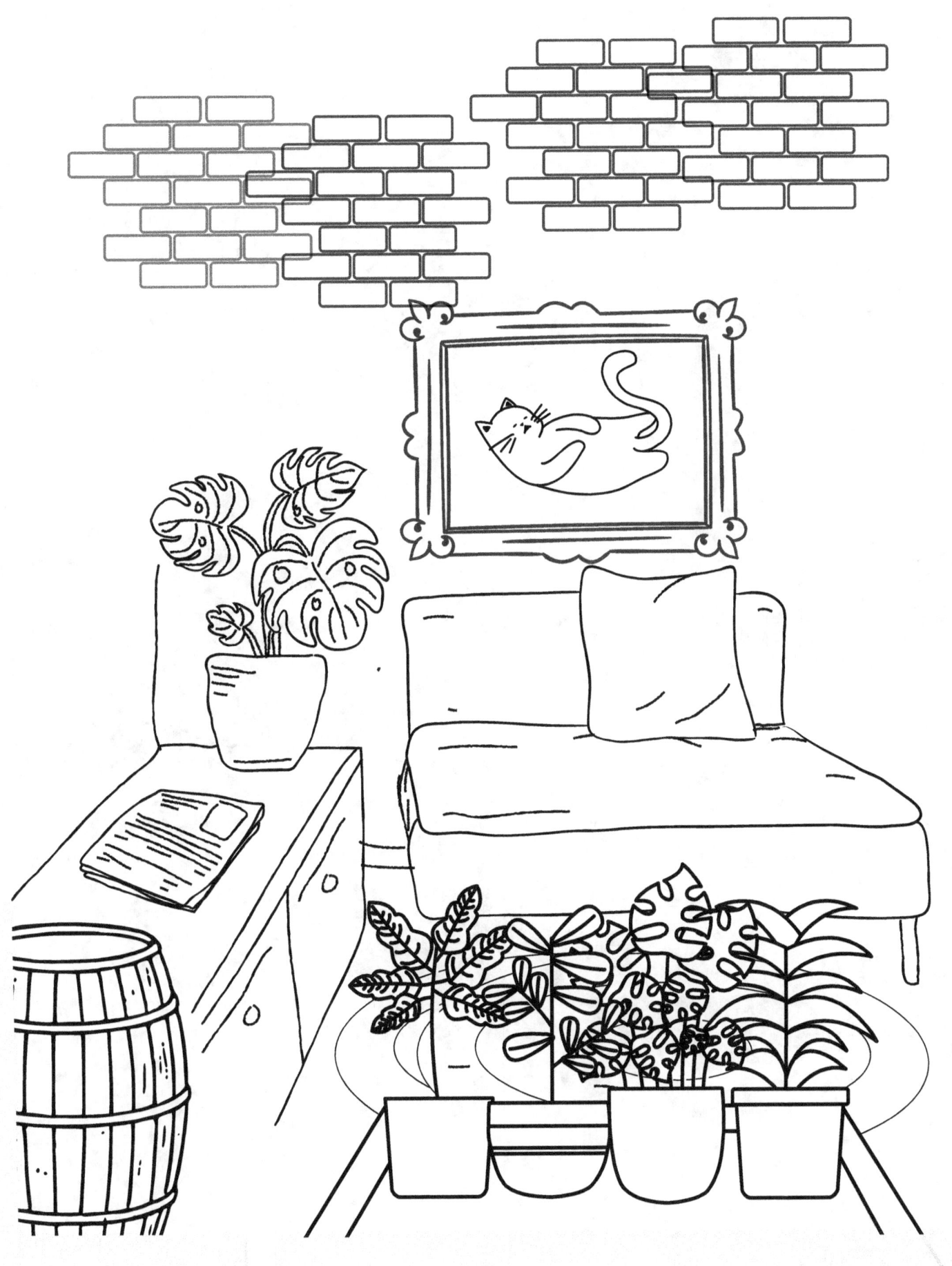

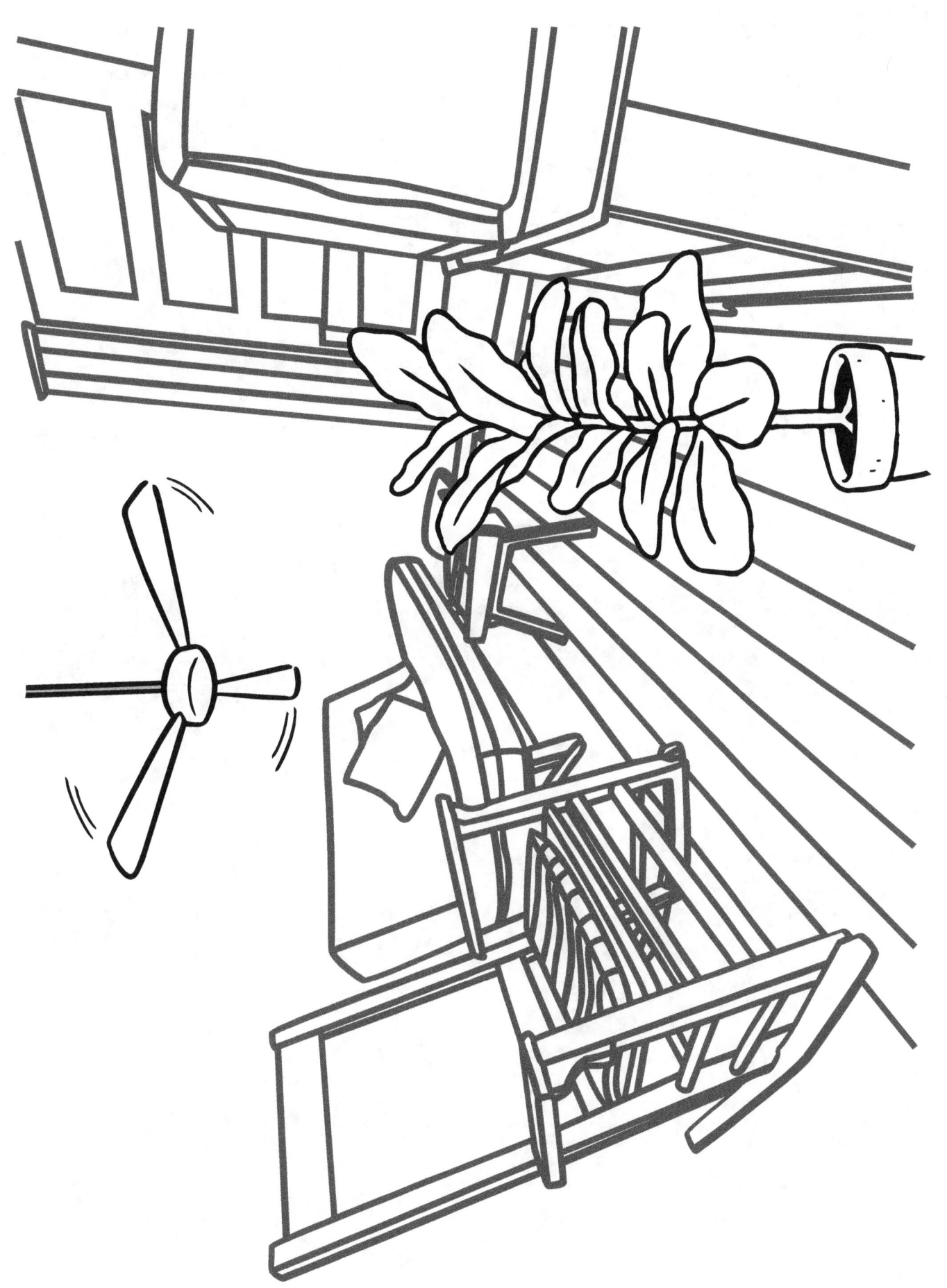

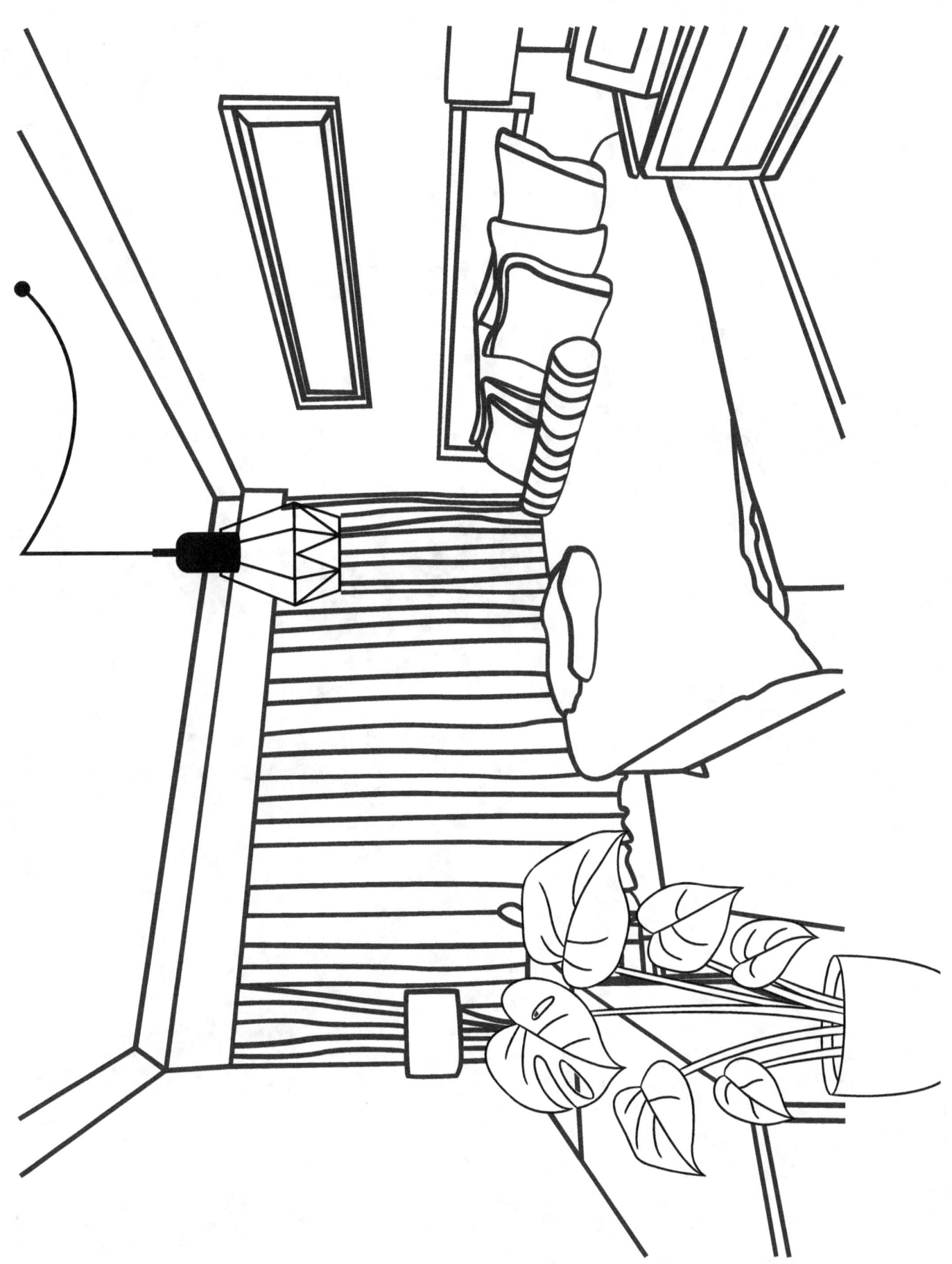

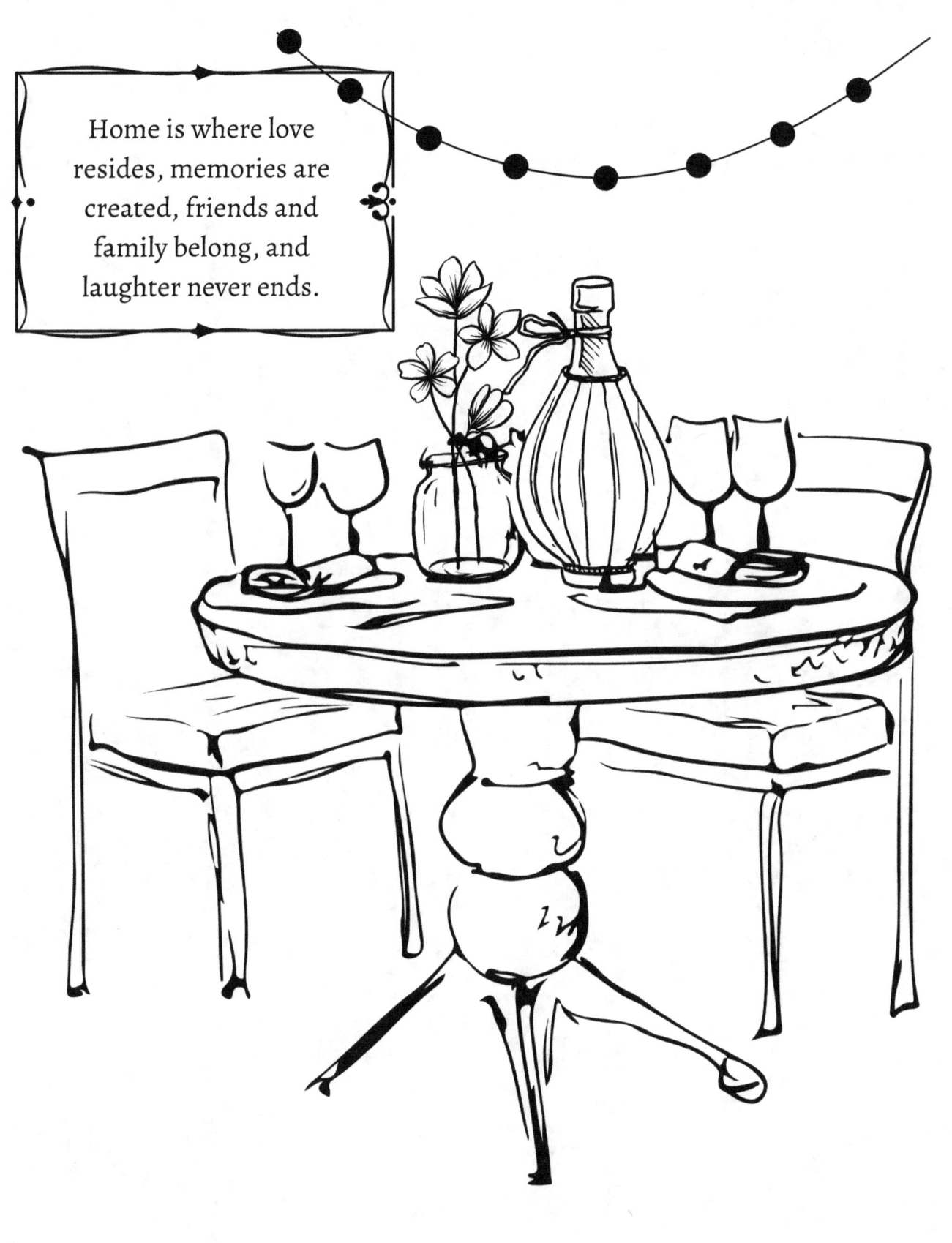

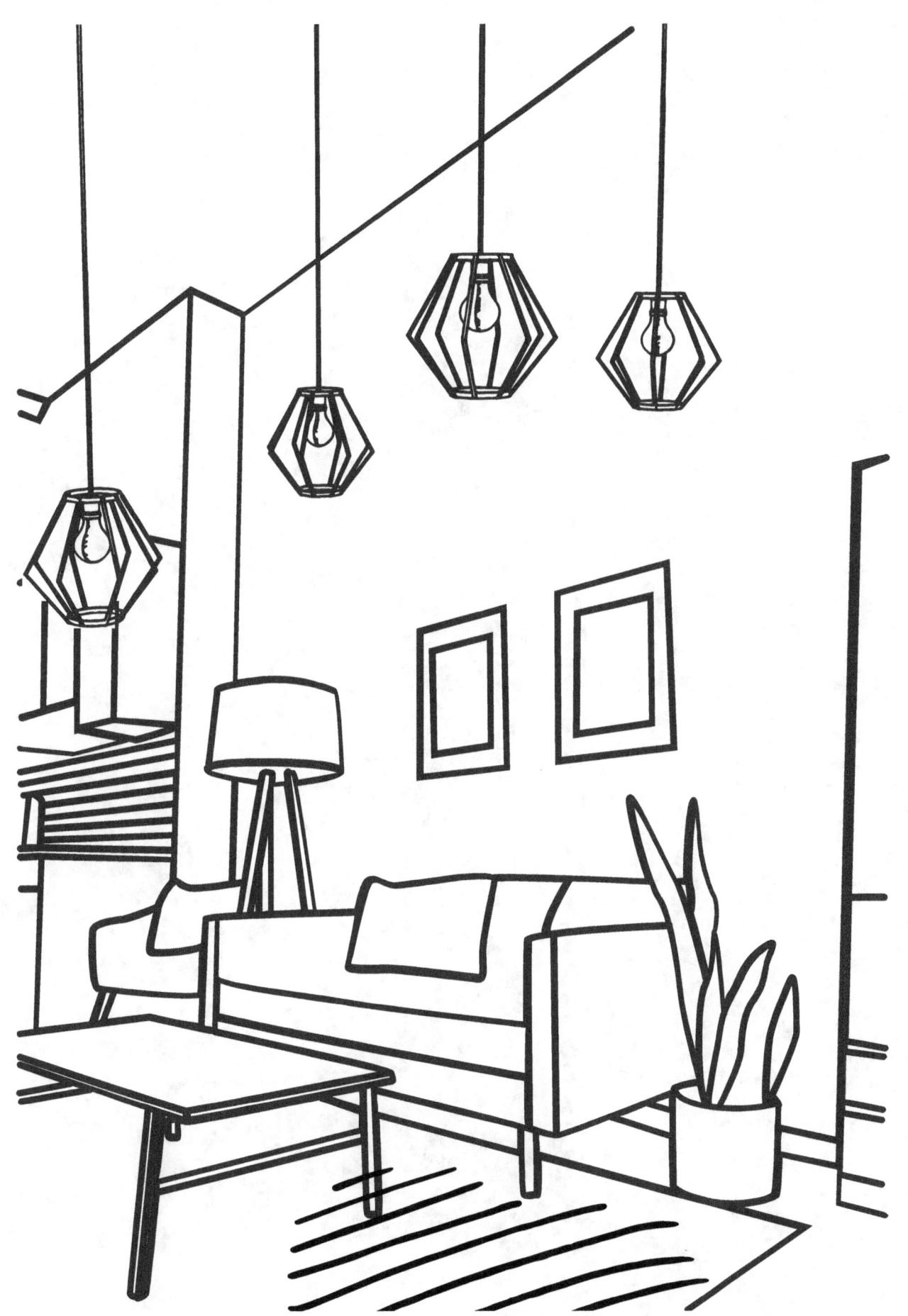

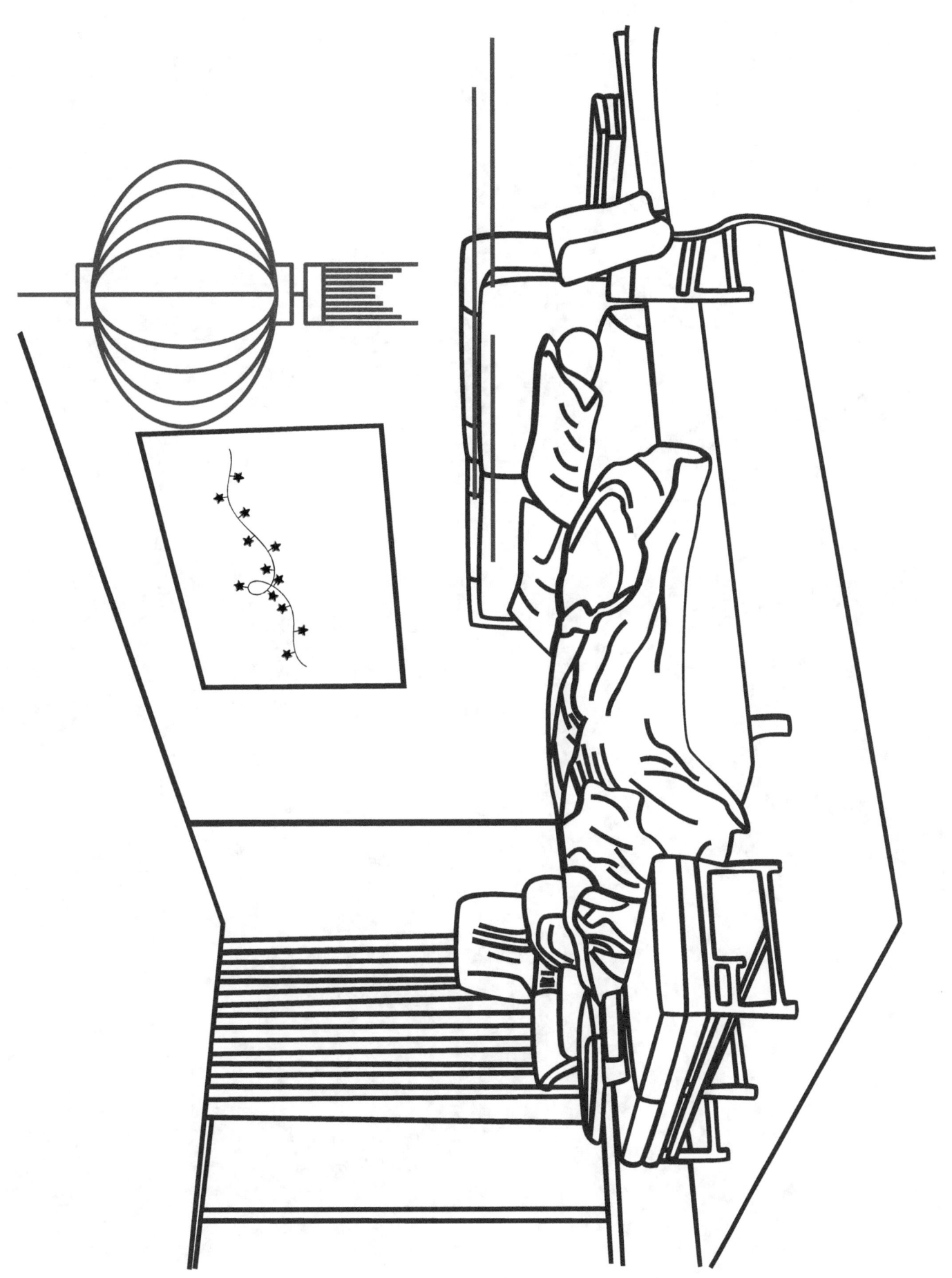

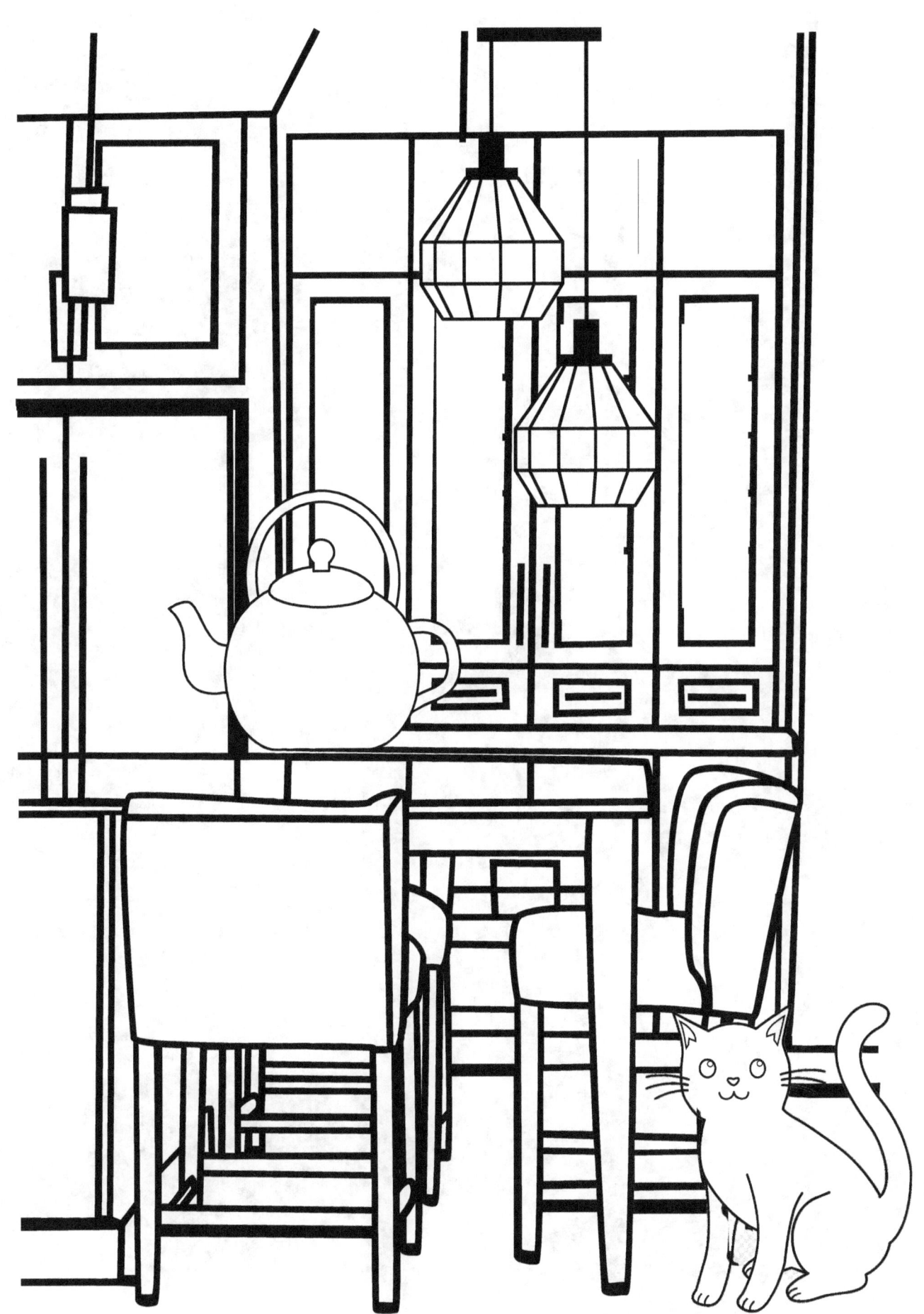

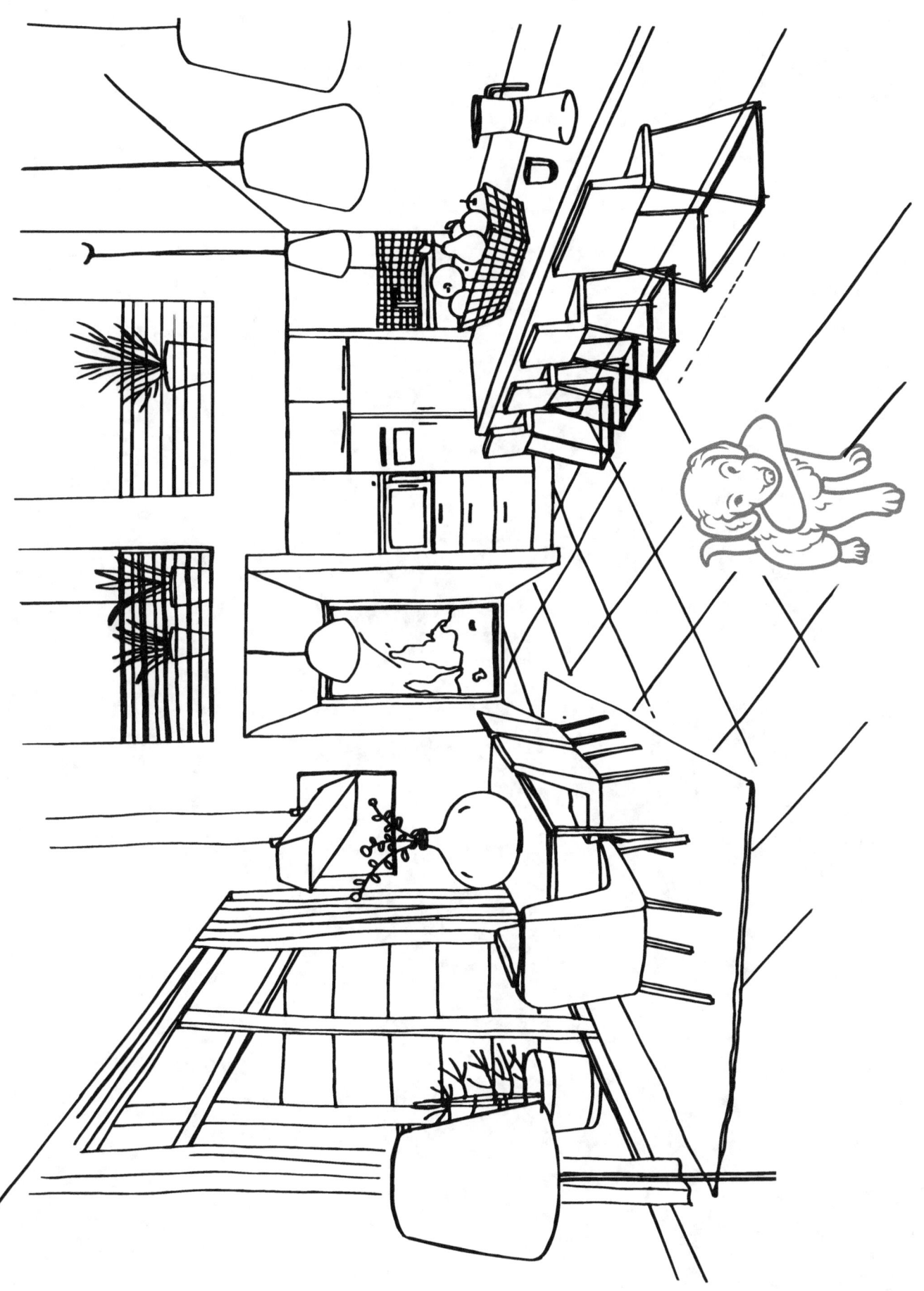

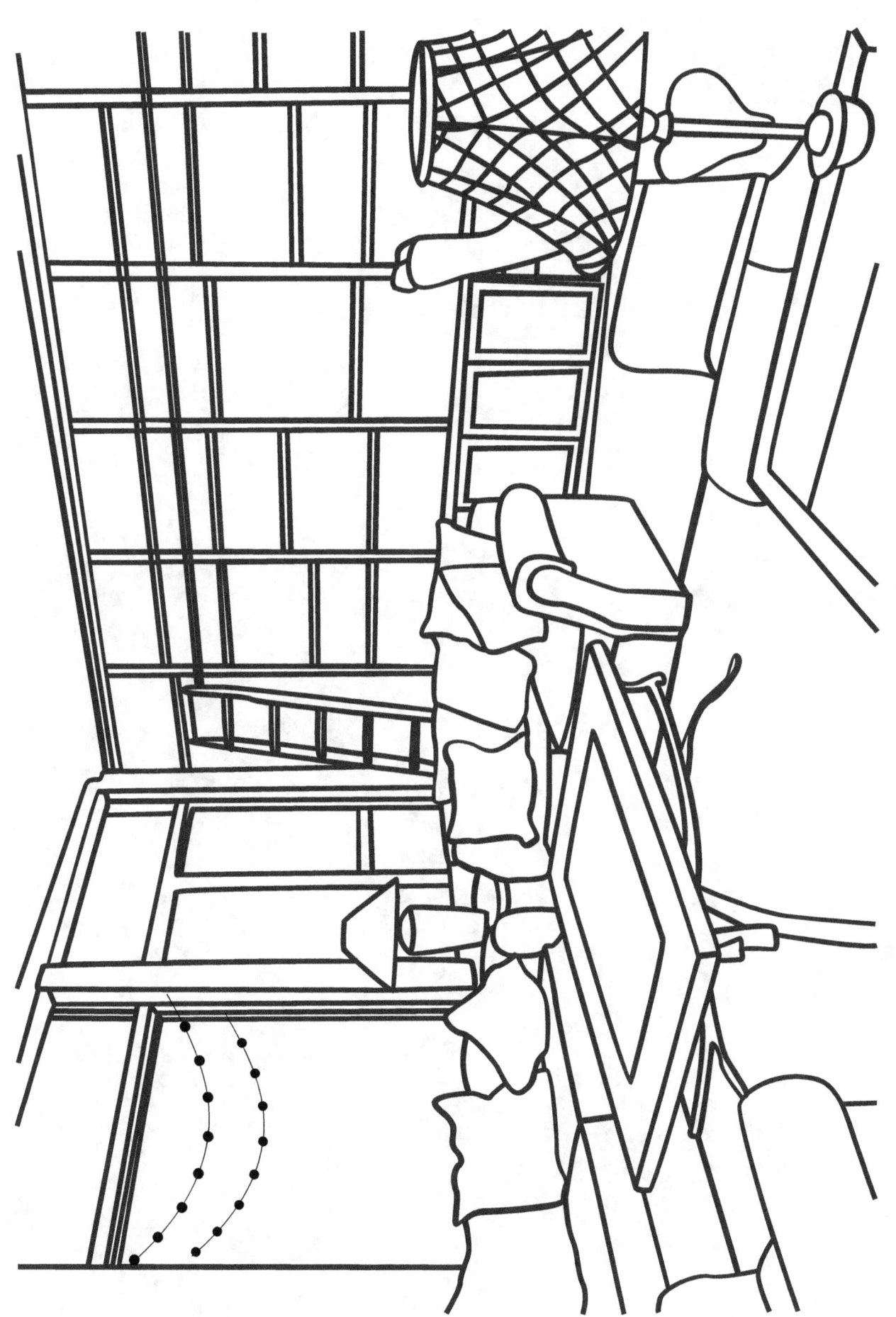

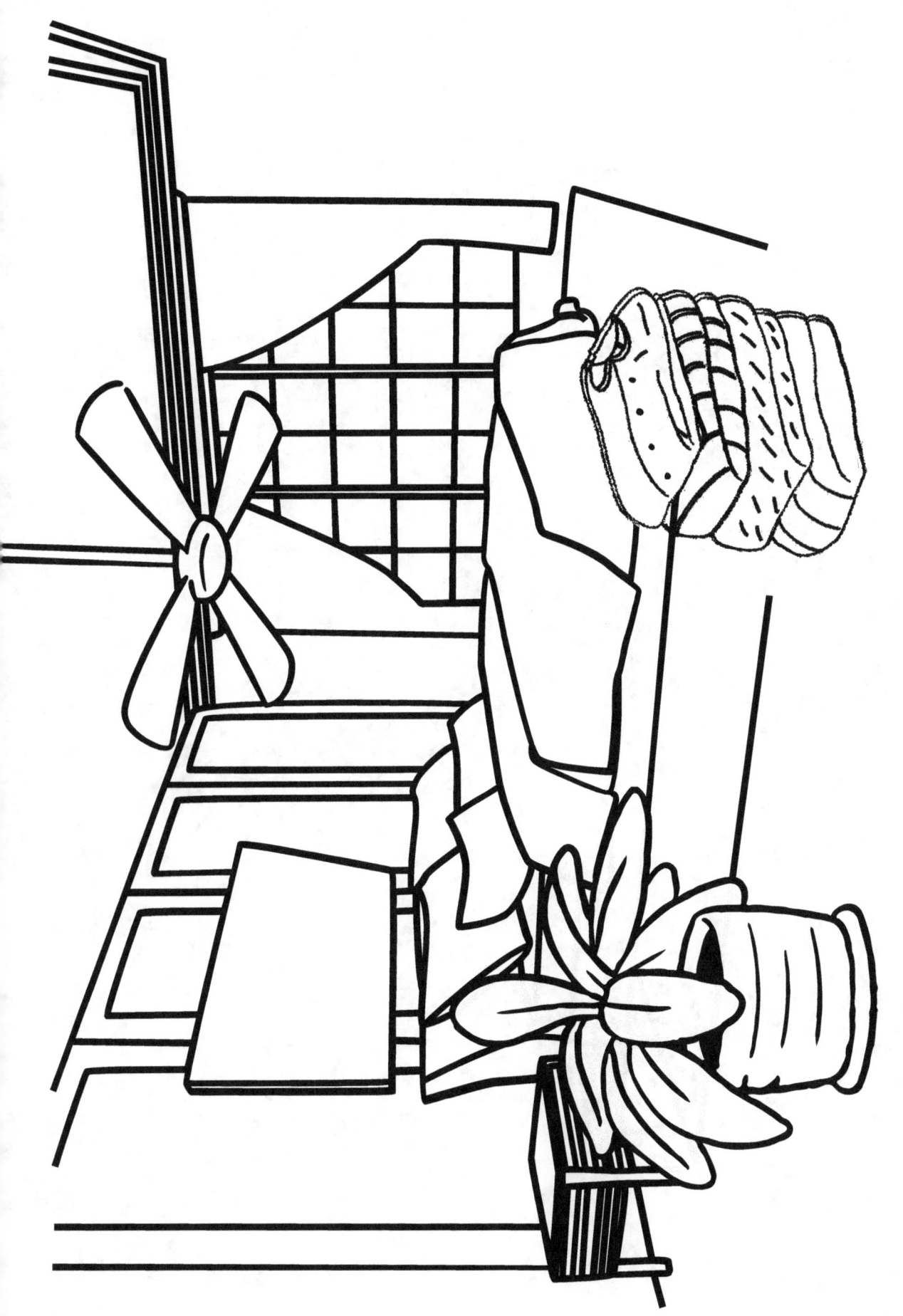

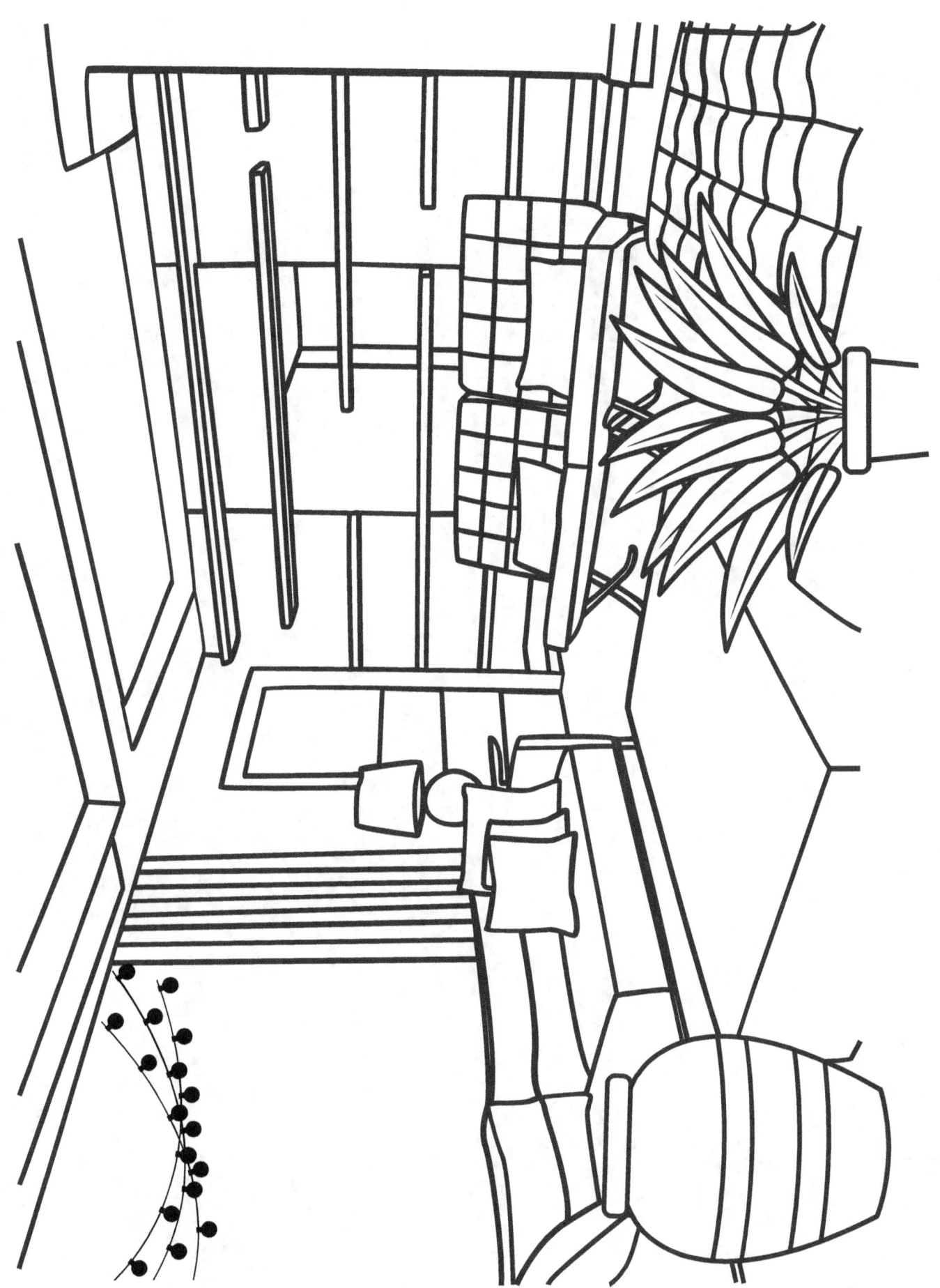

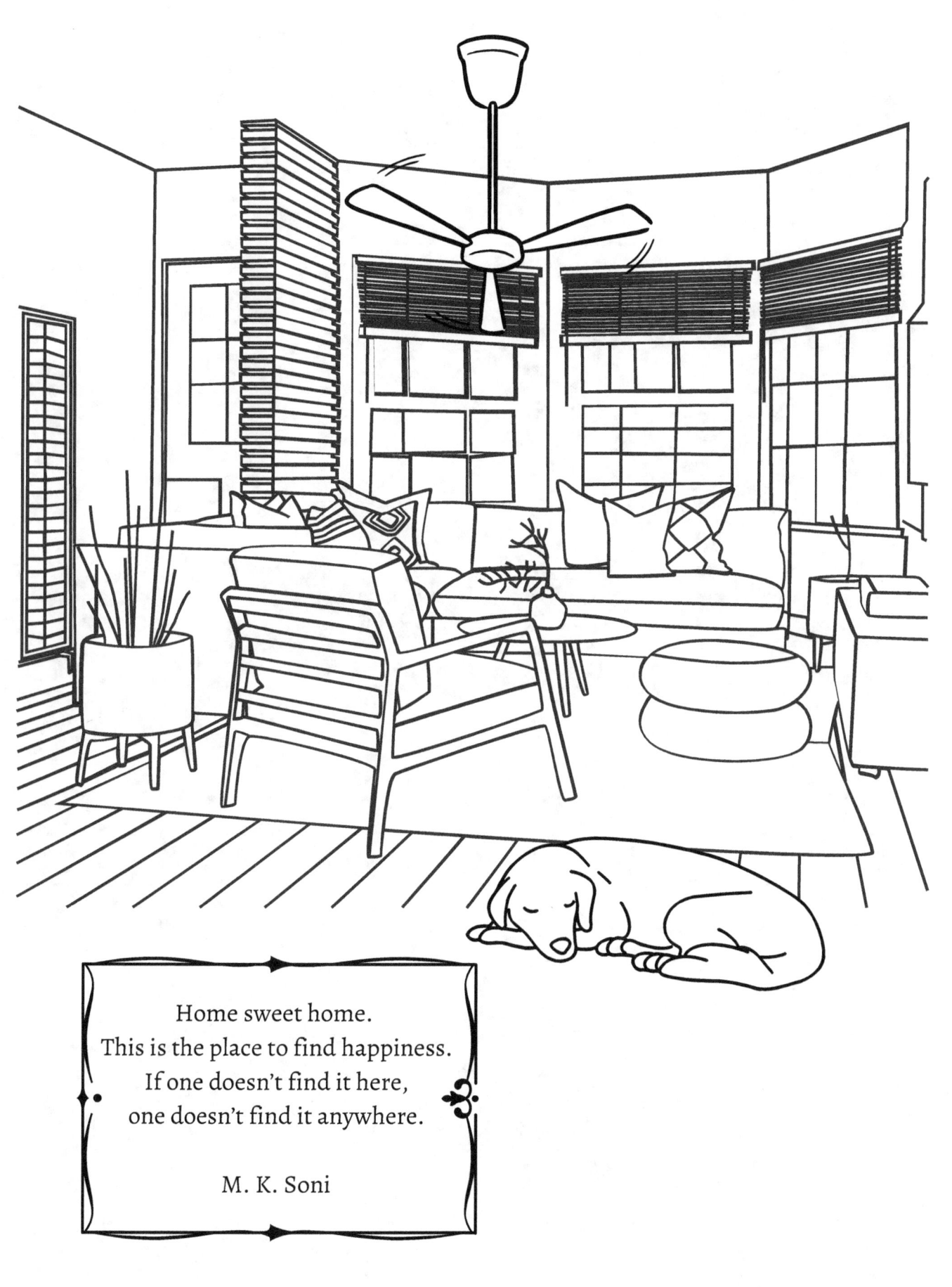

Home sweet home.
This is the place to find happiness.
If one doesn't find it here,
one doesn't find it anywhere.

M. K. Soni

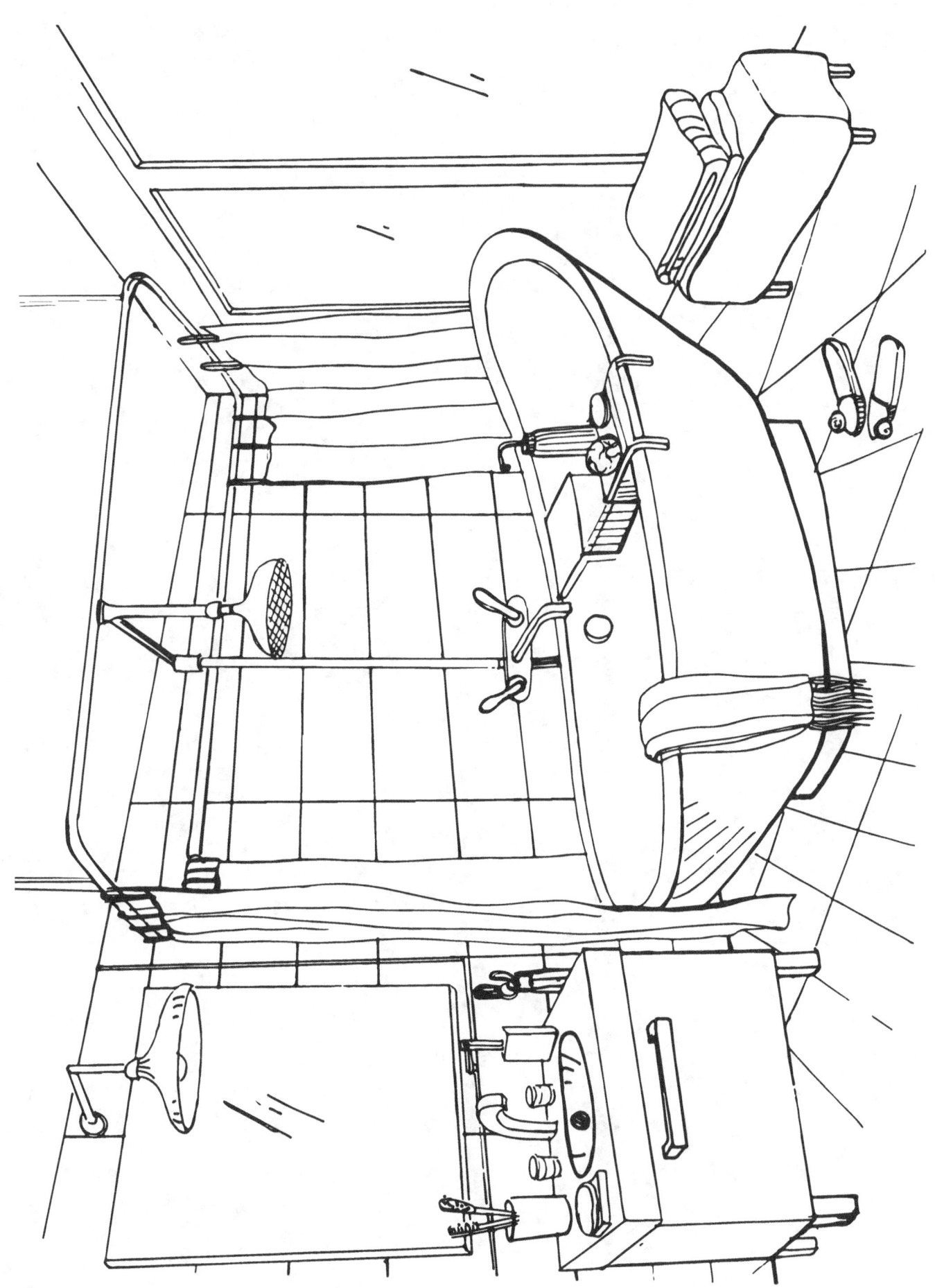

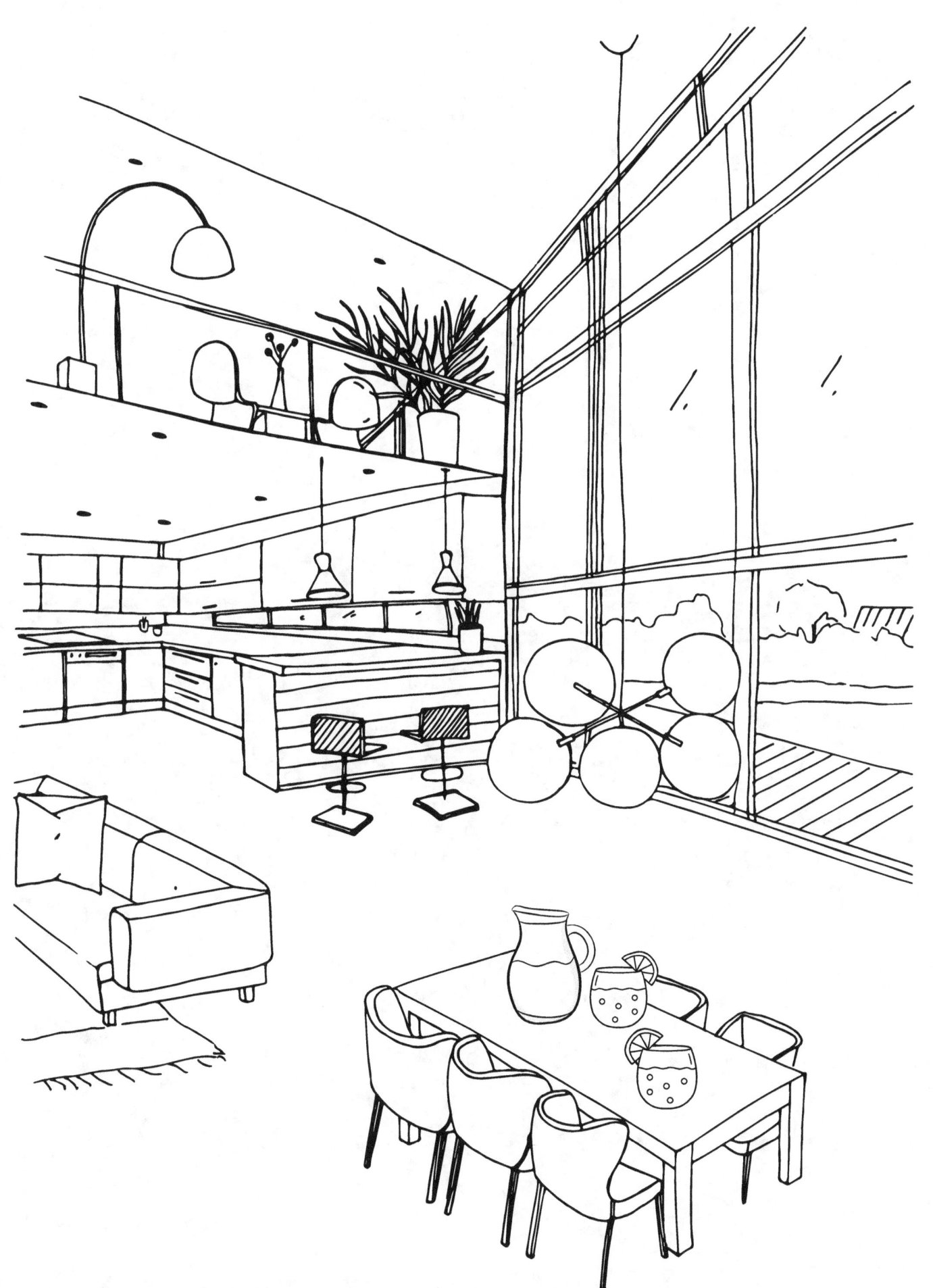

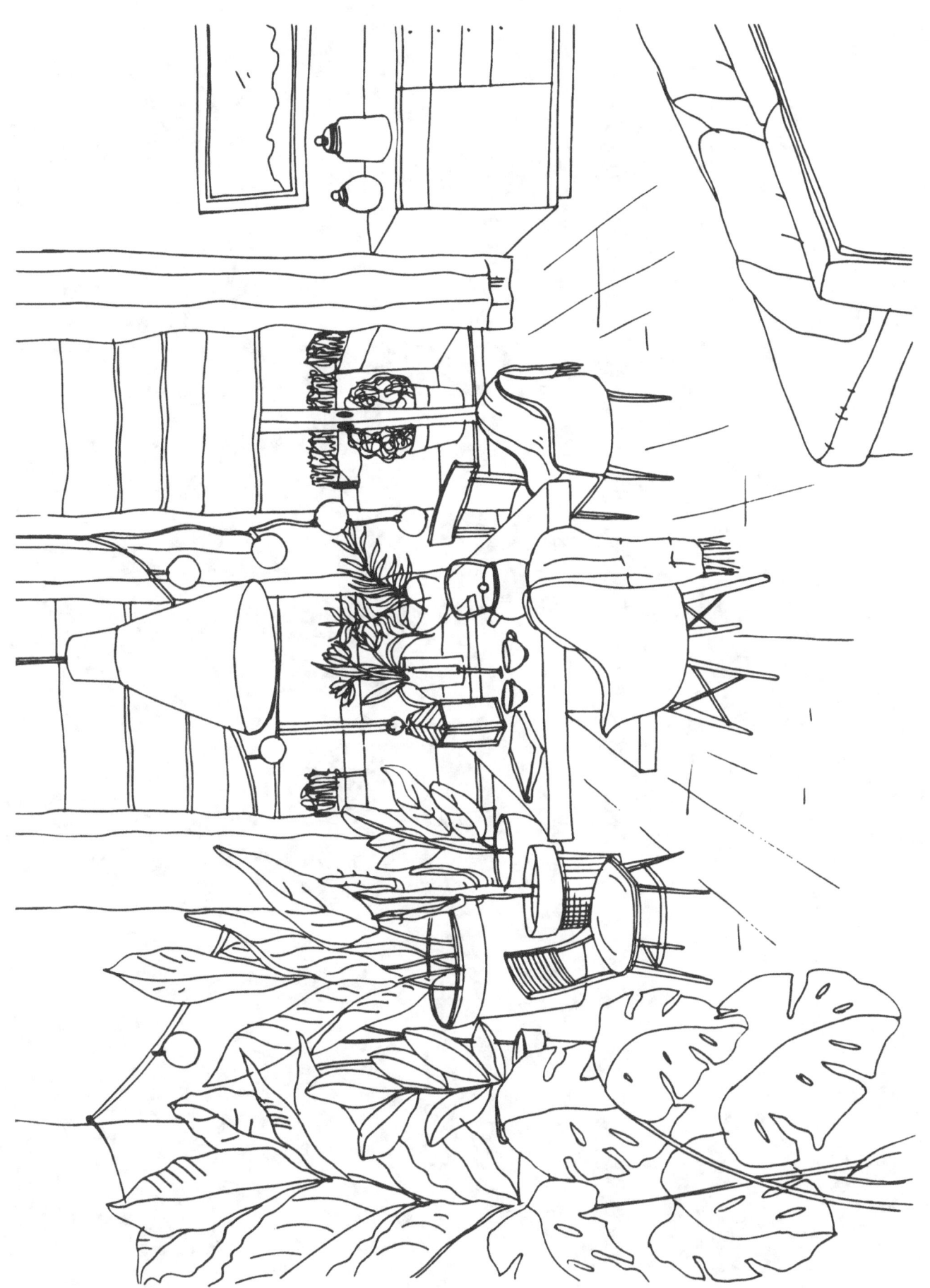

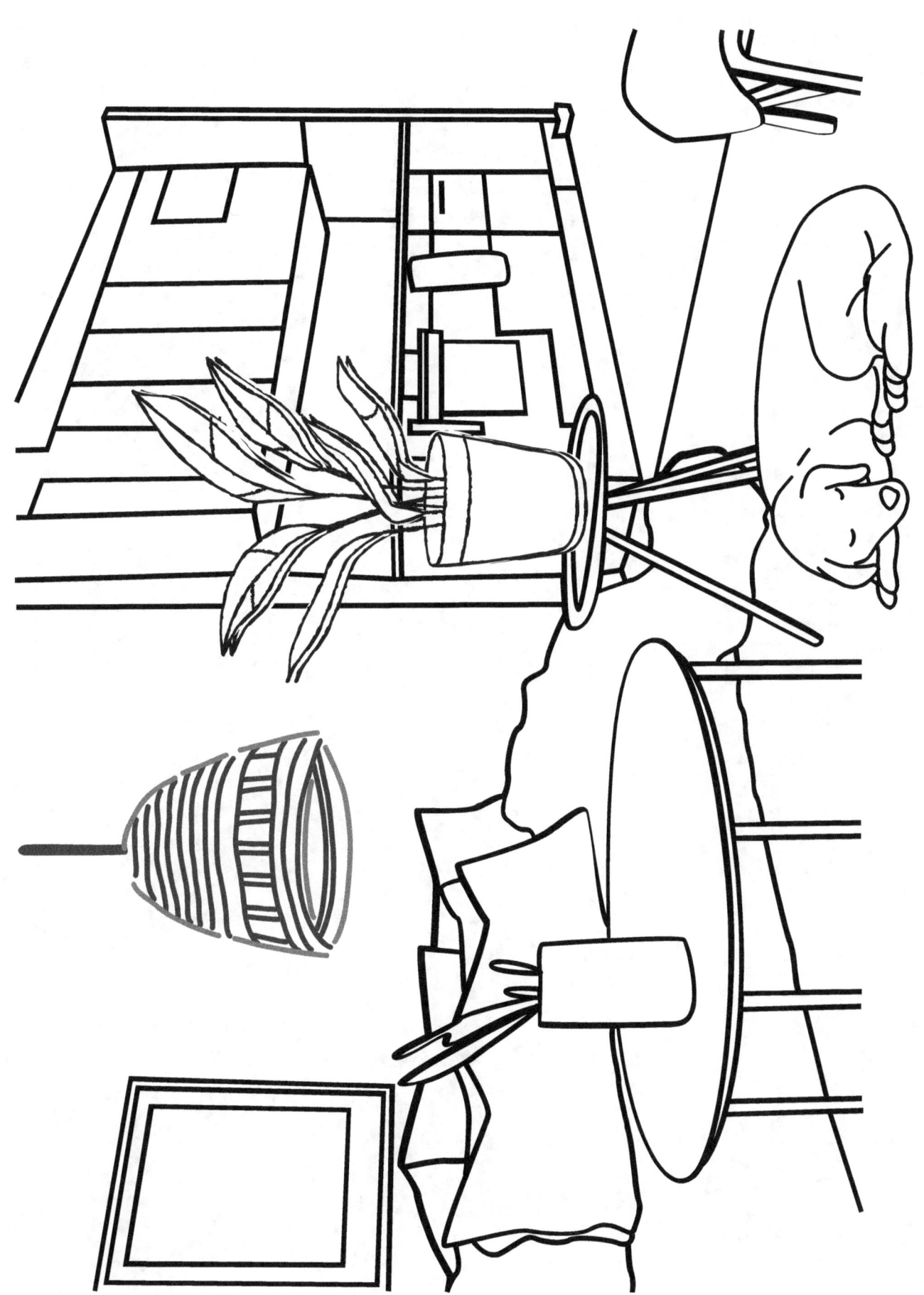

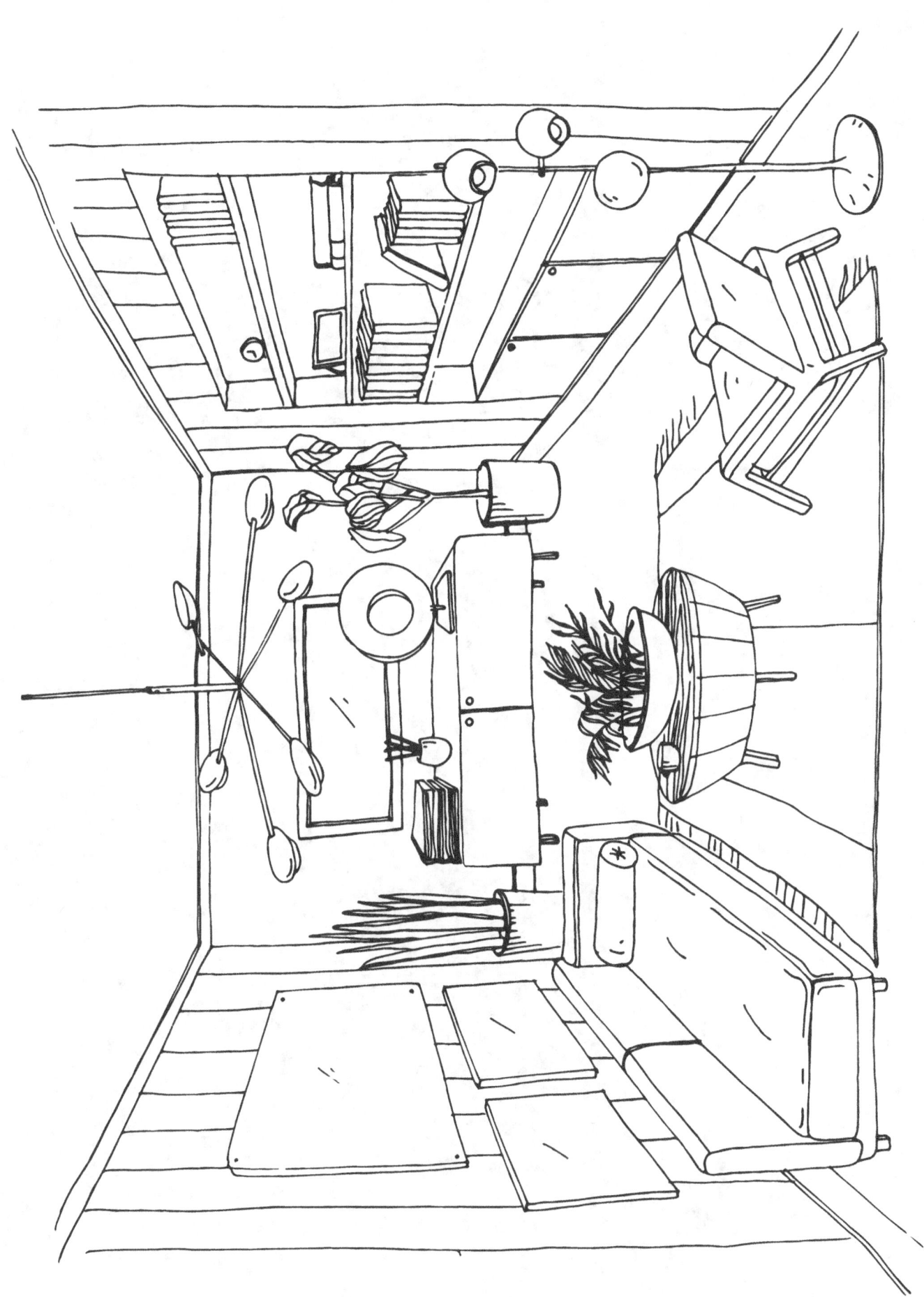

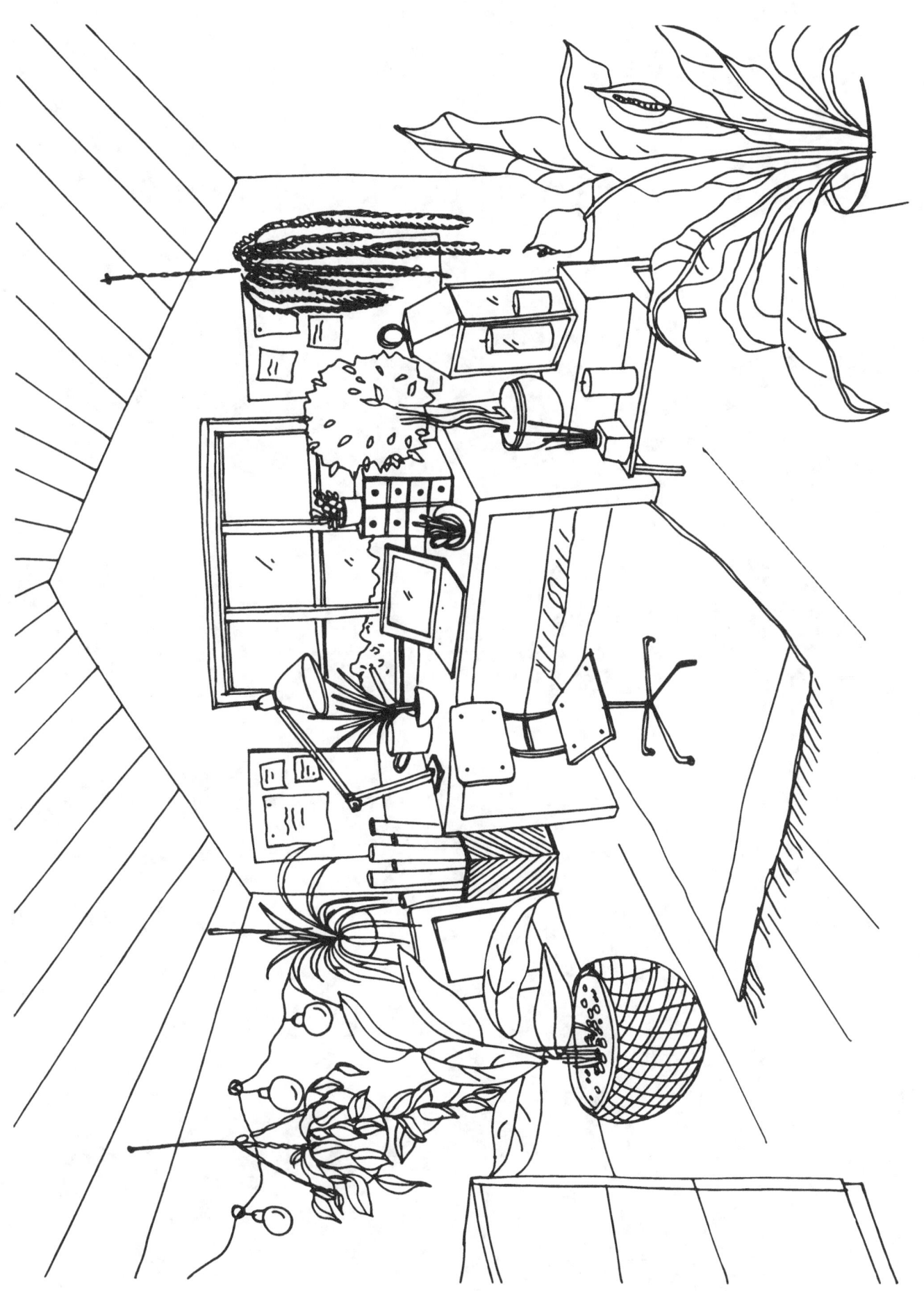

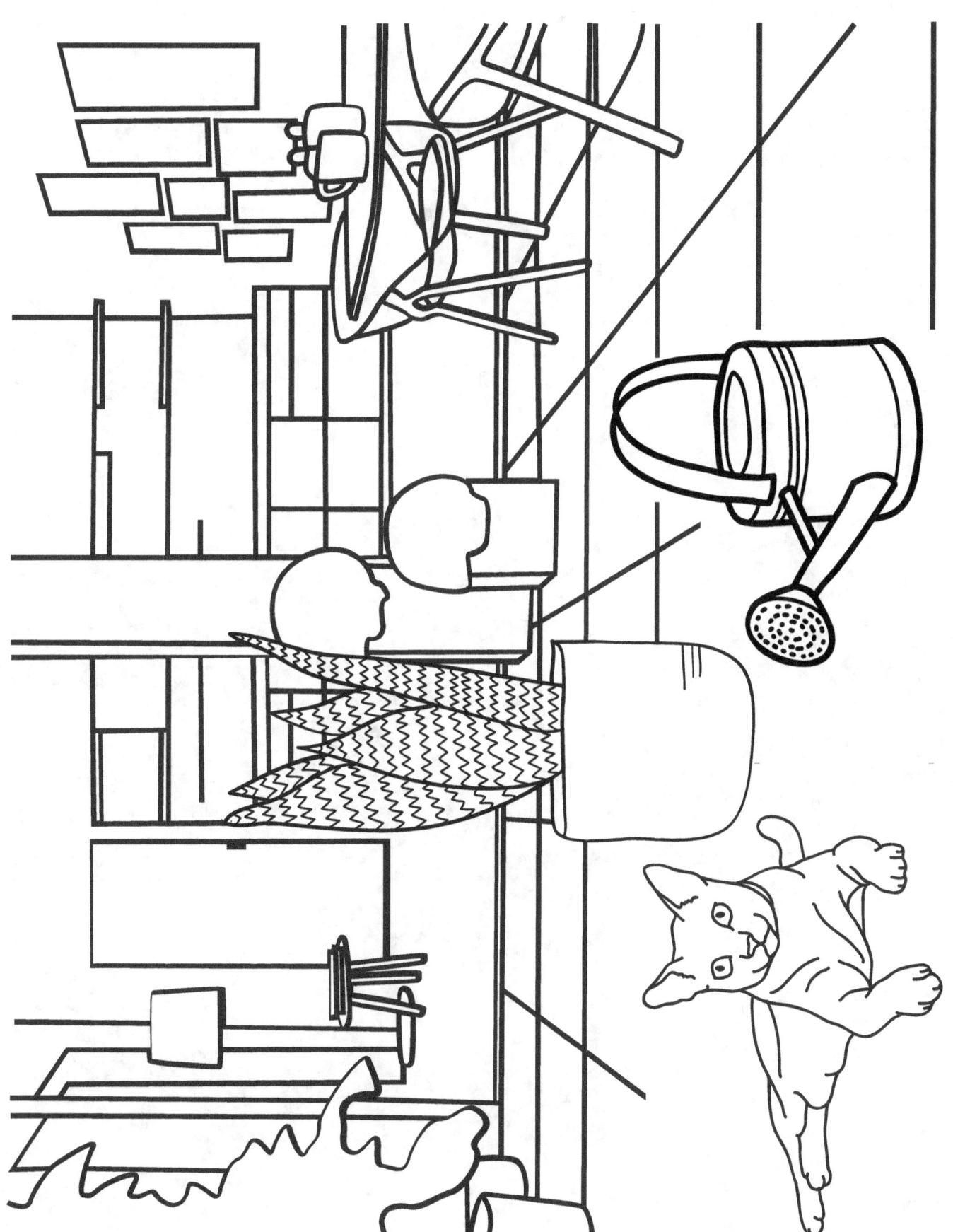

> The magic thing about home is that it feels good to leave, and it feels even better to come back.

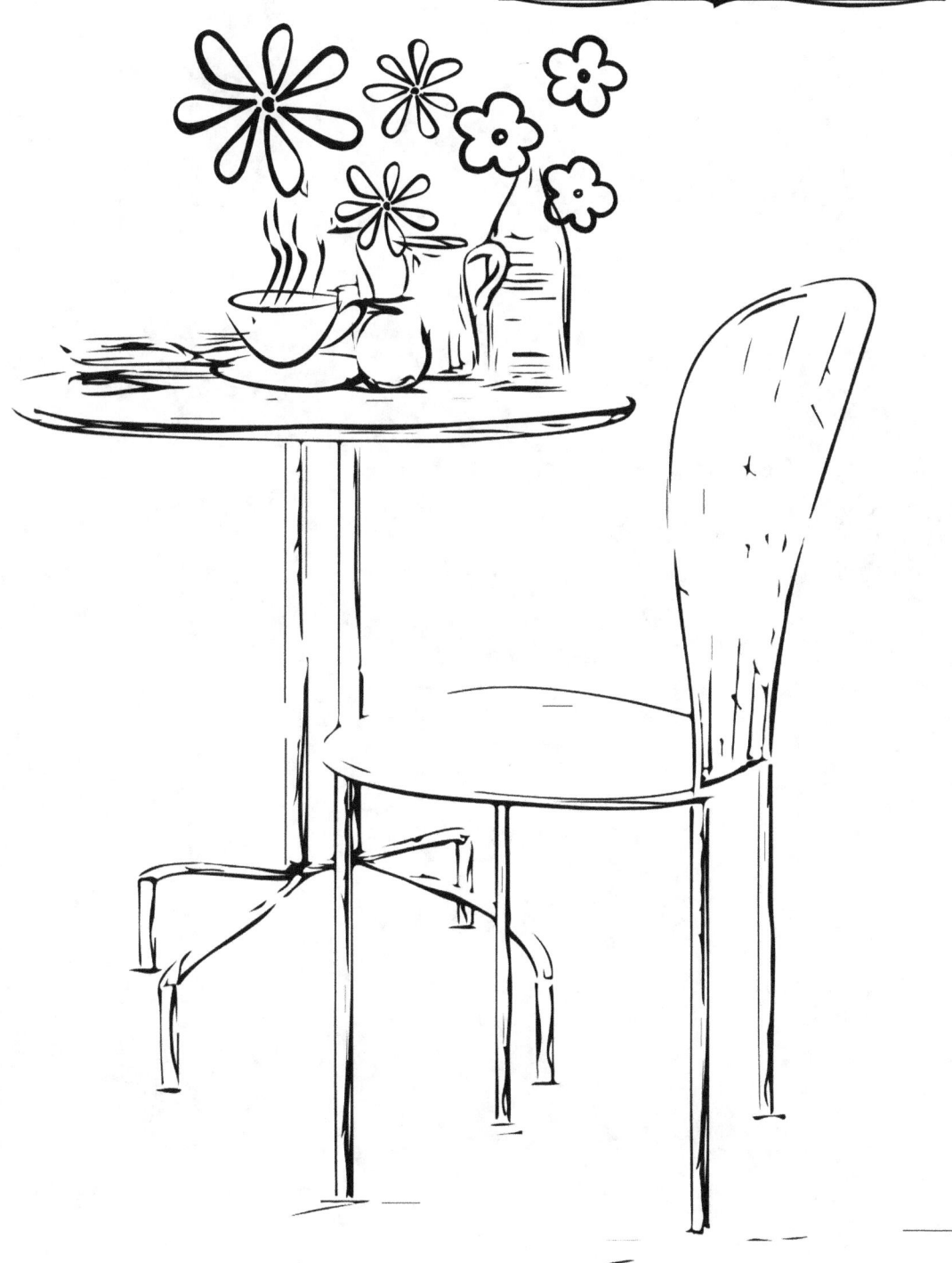

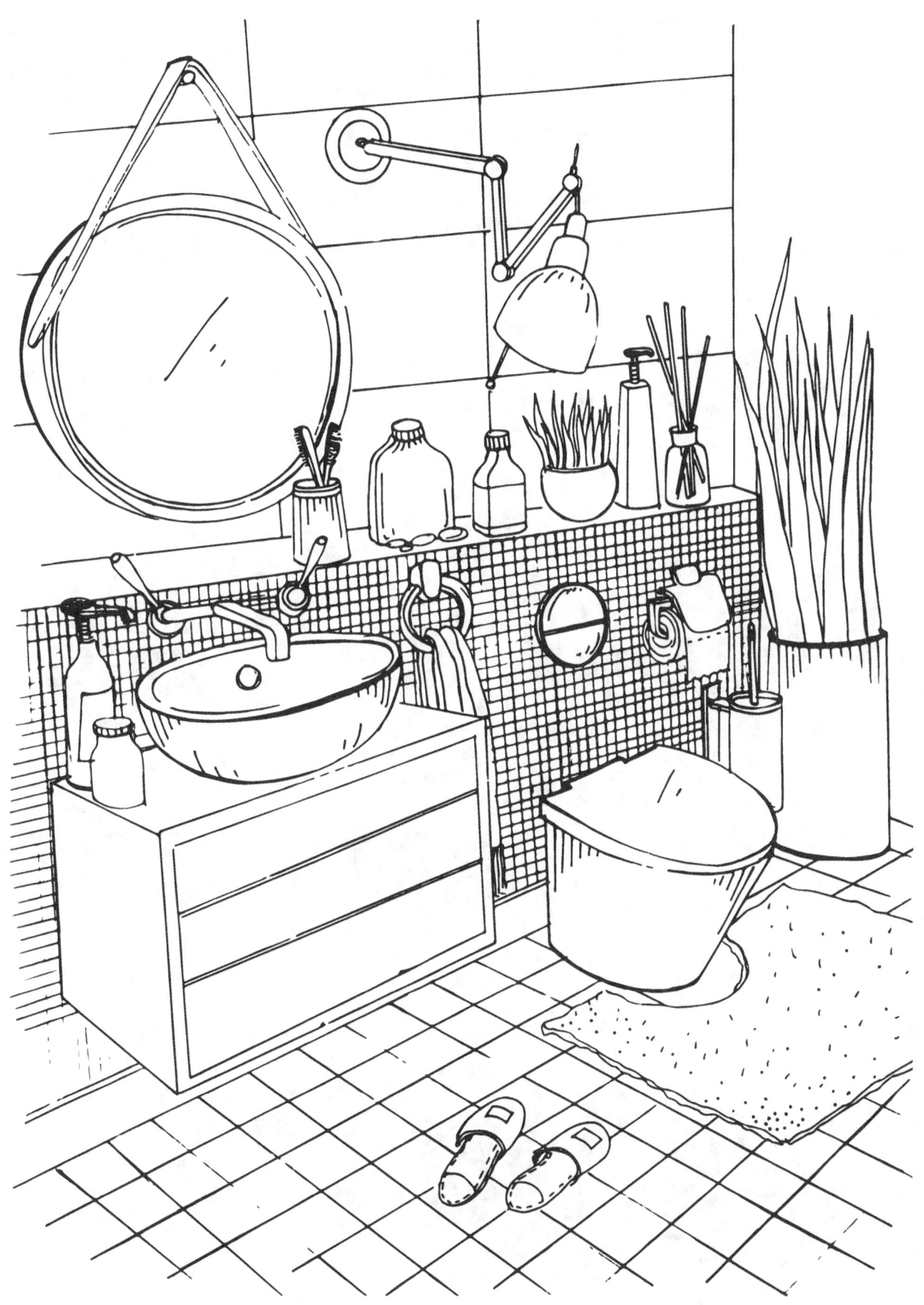

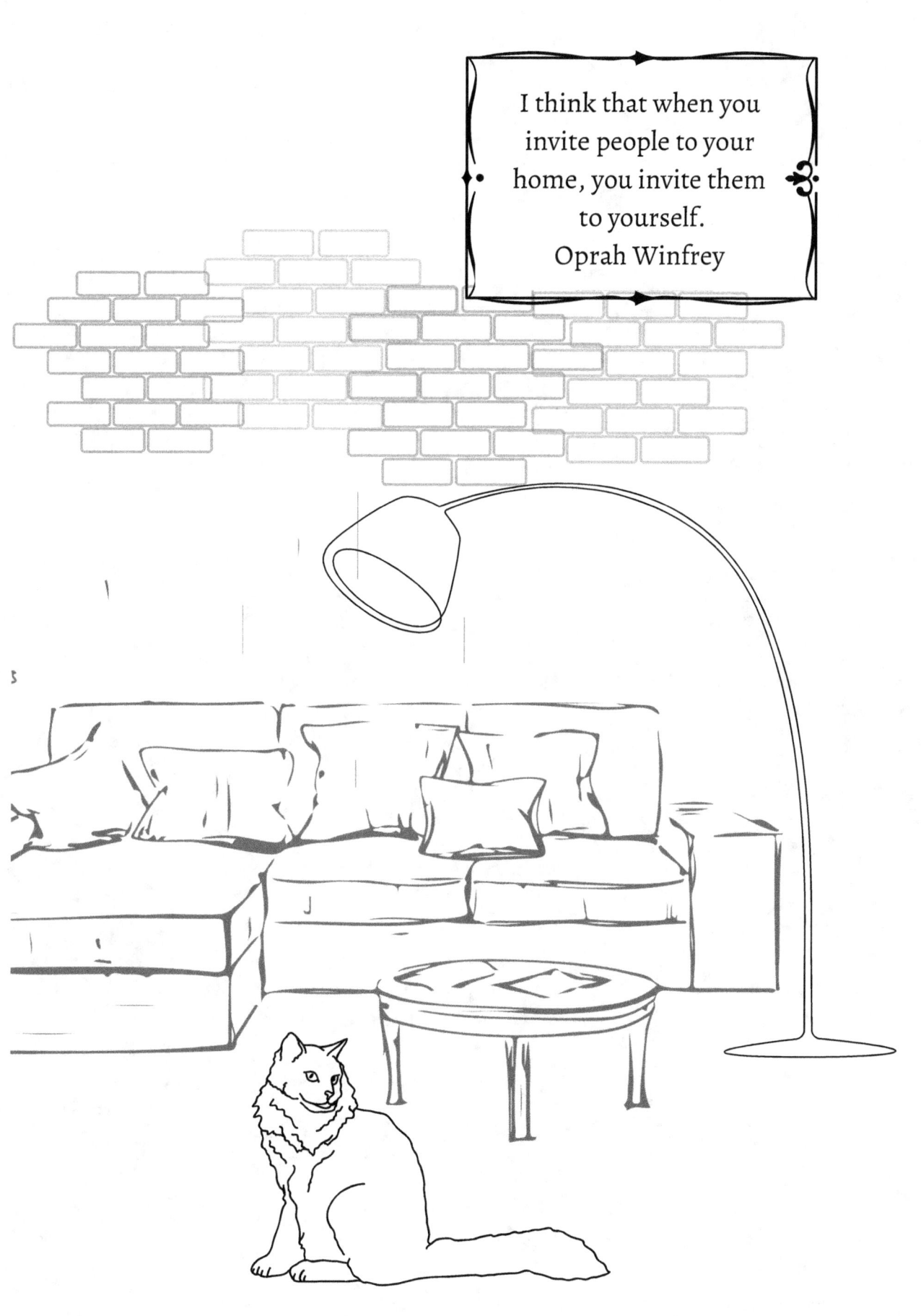

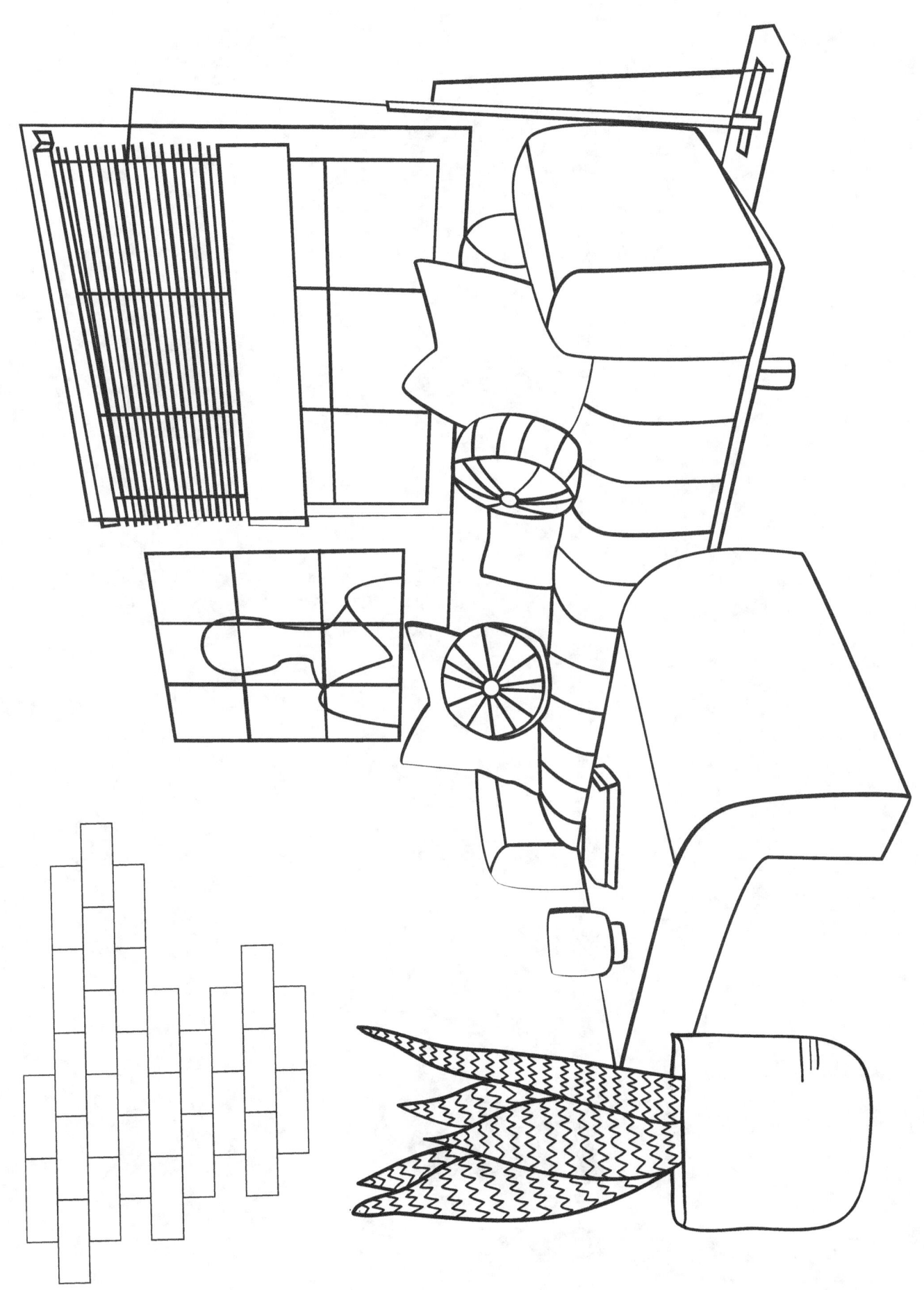

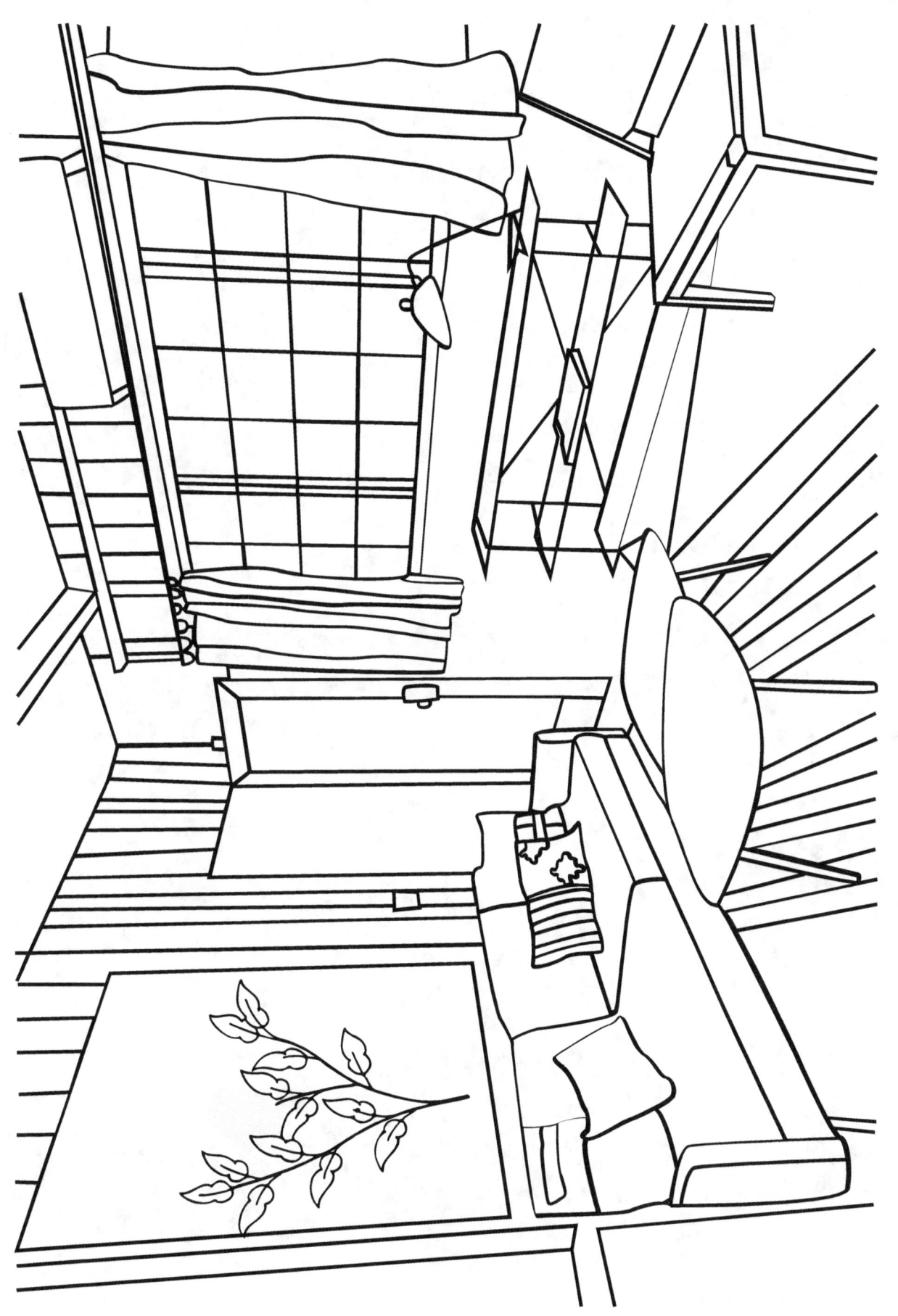

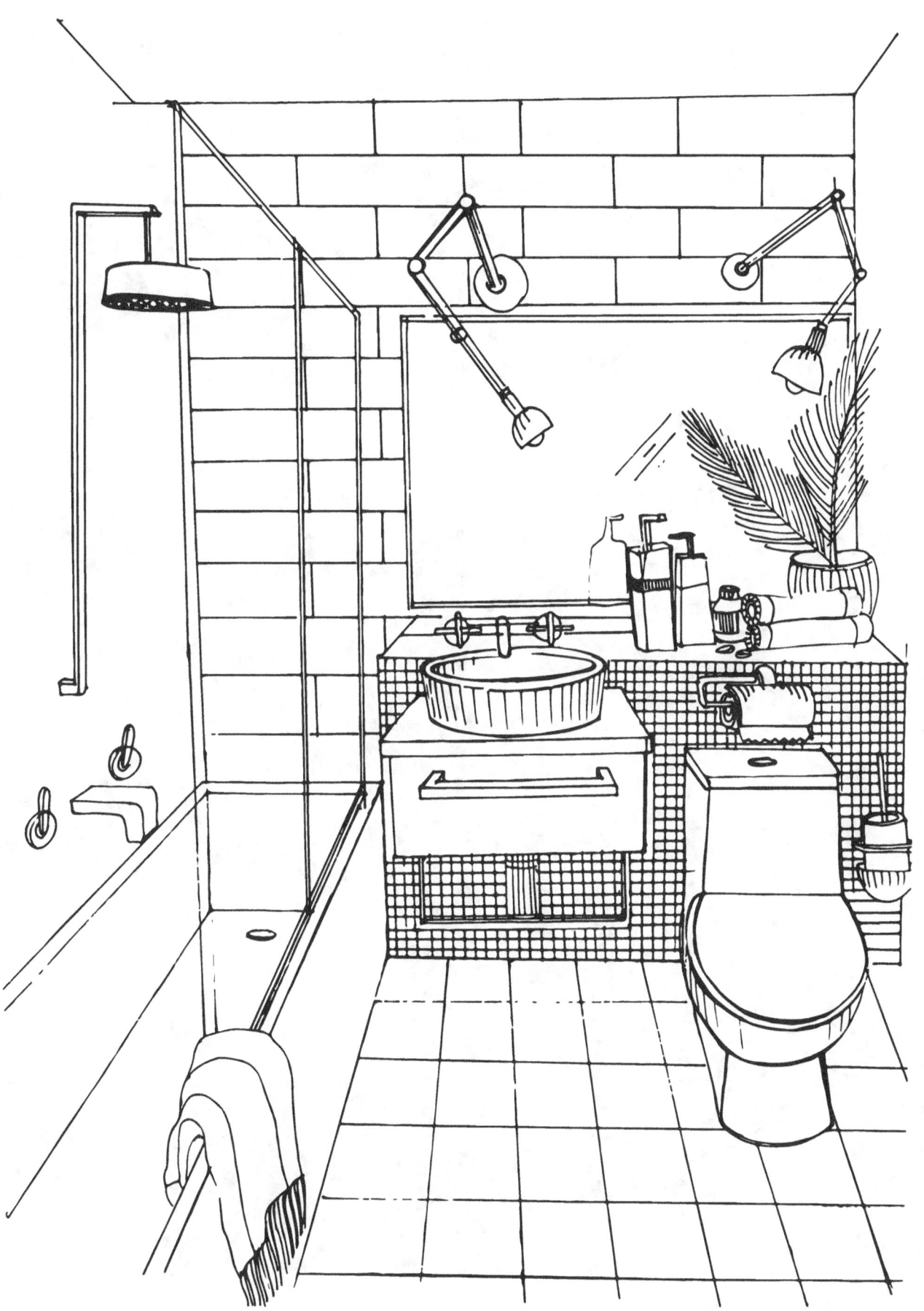

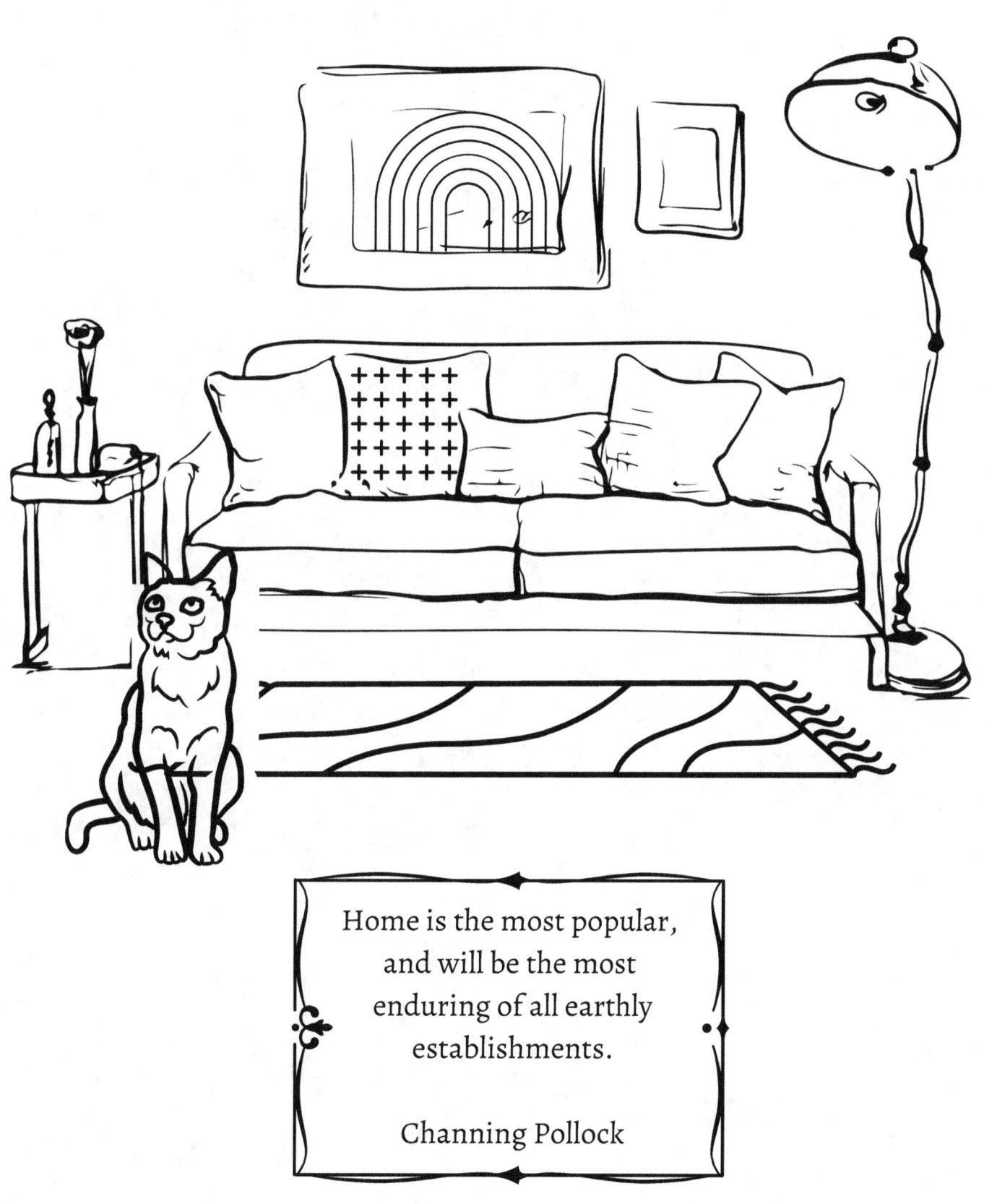

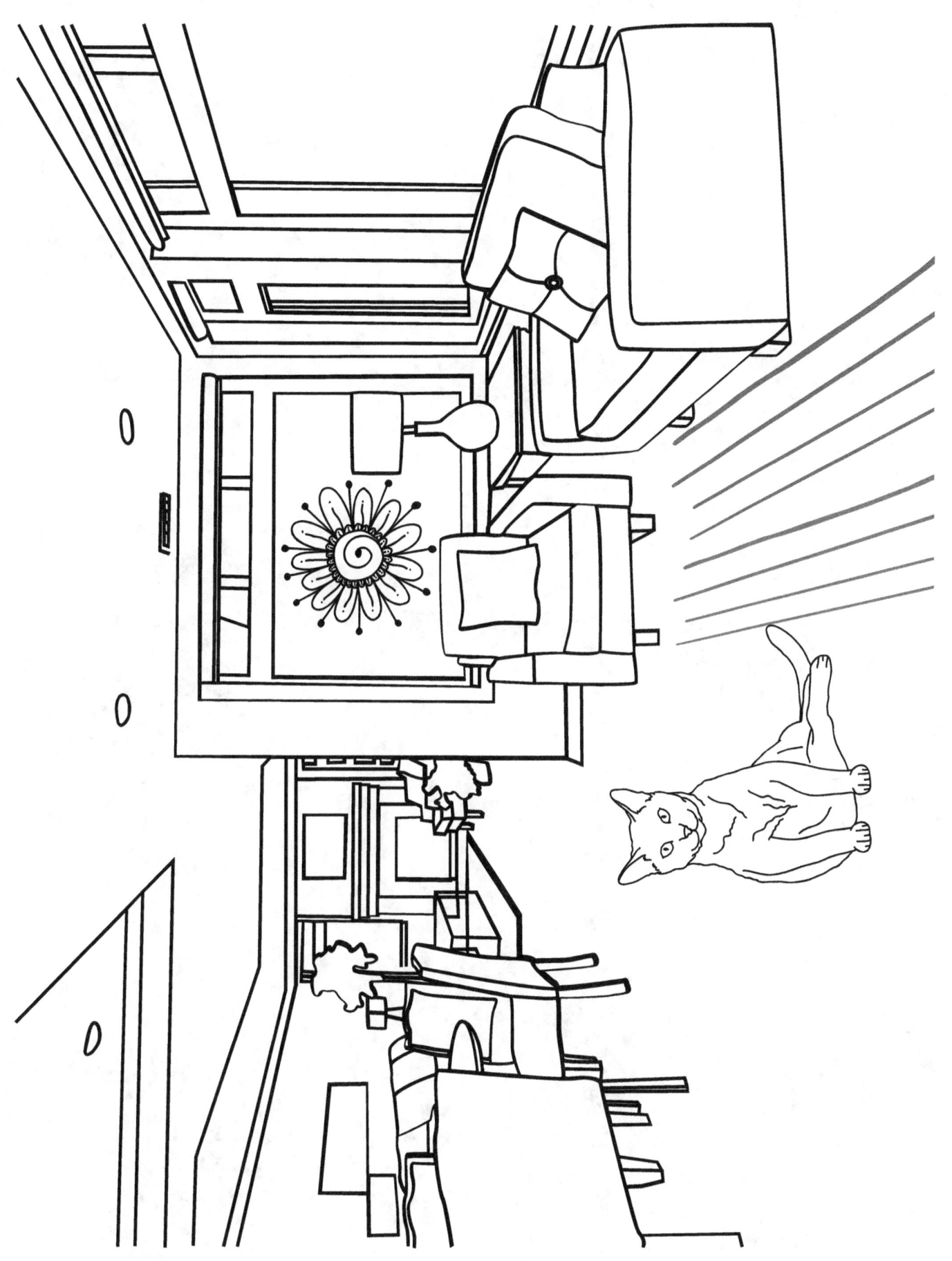

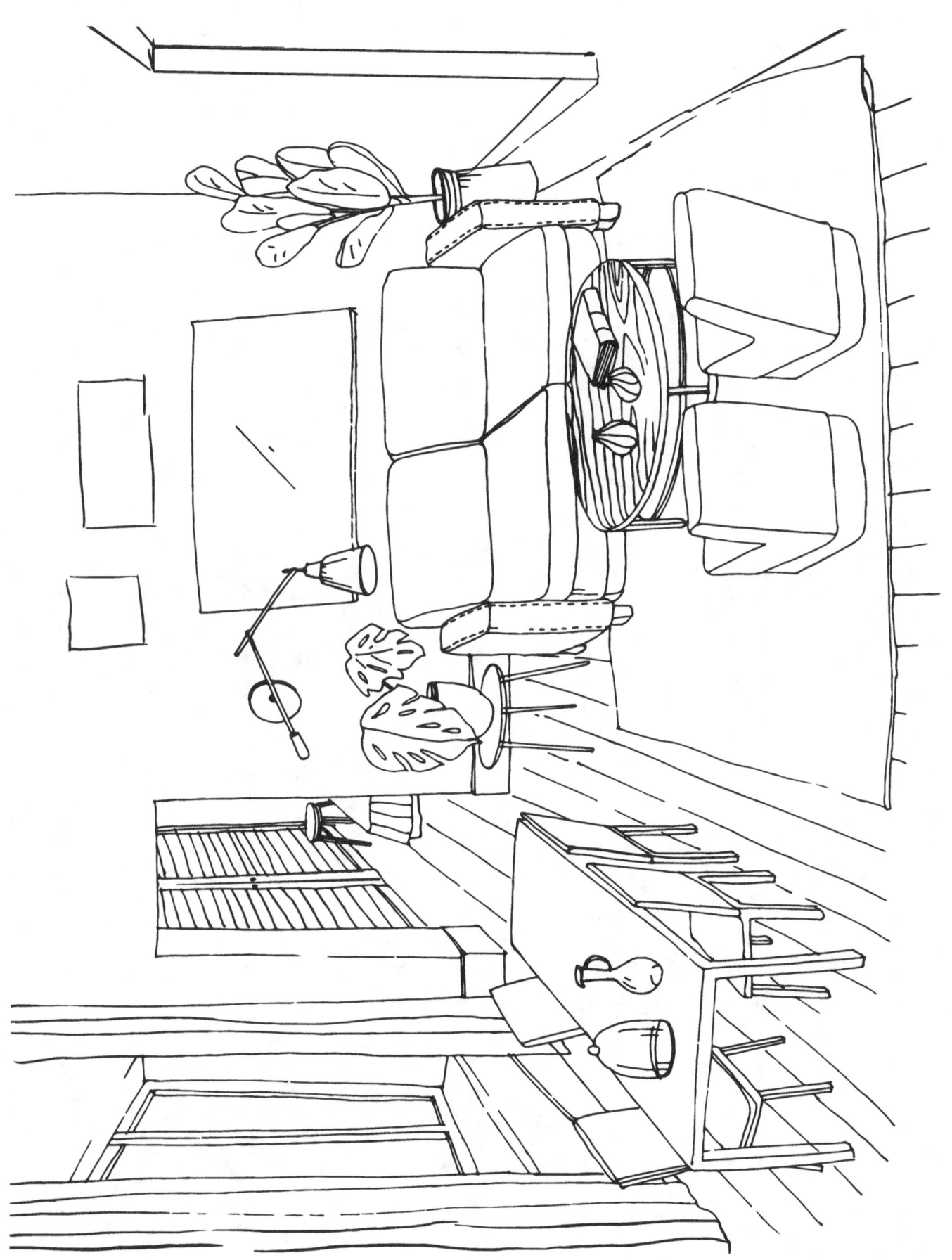

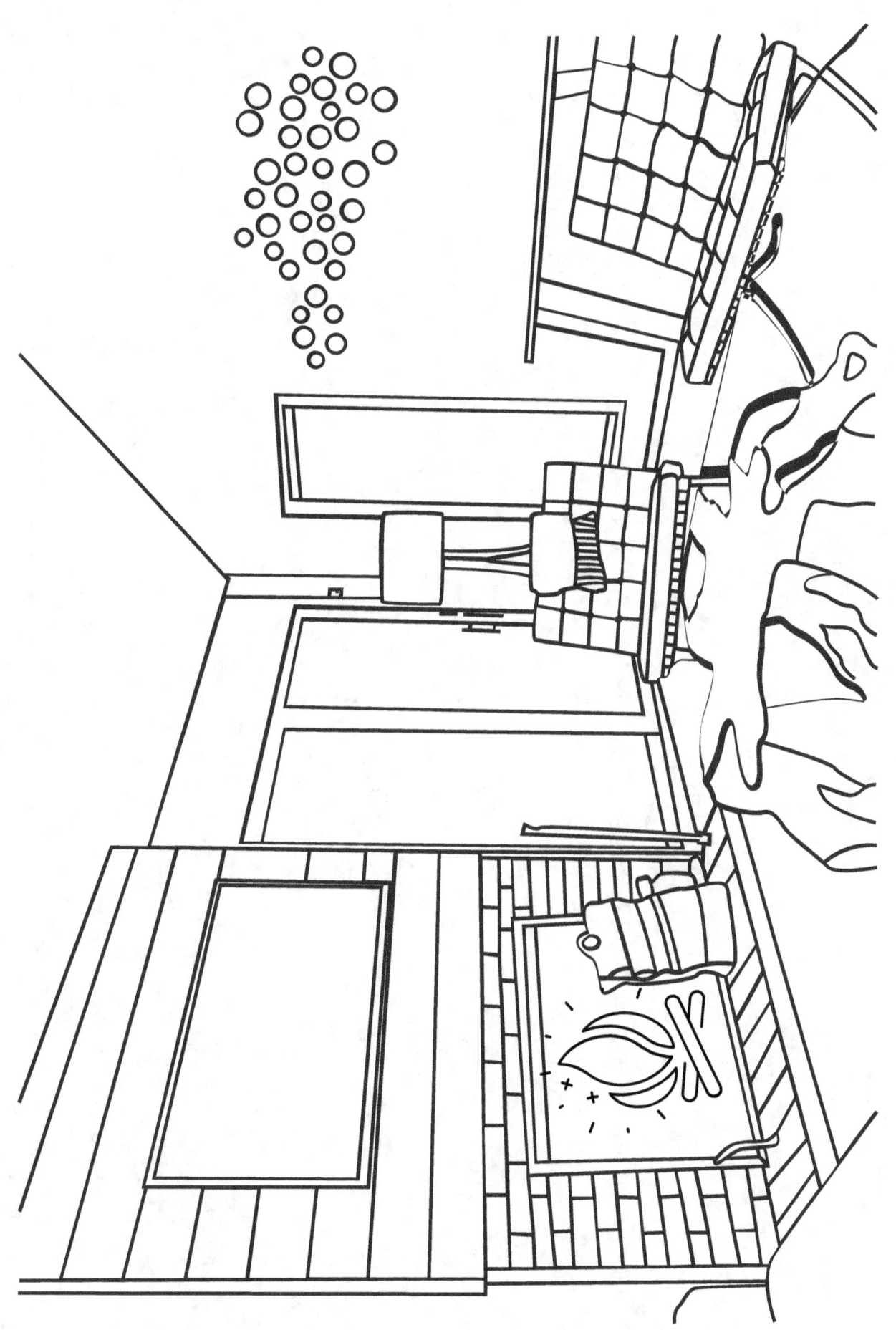

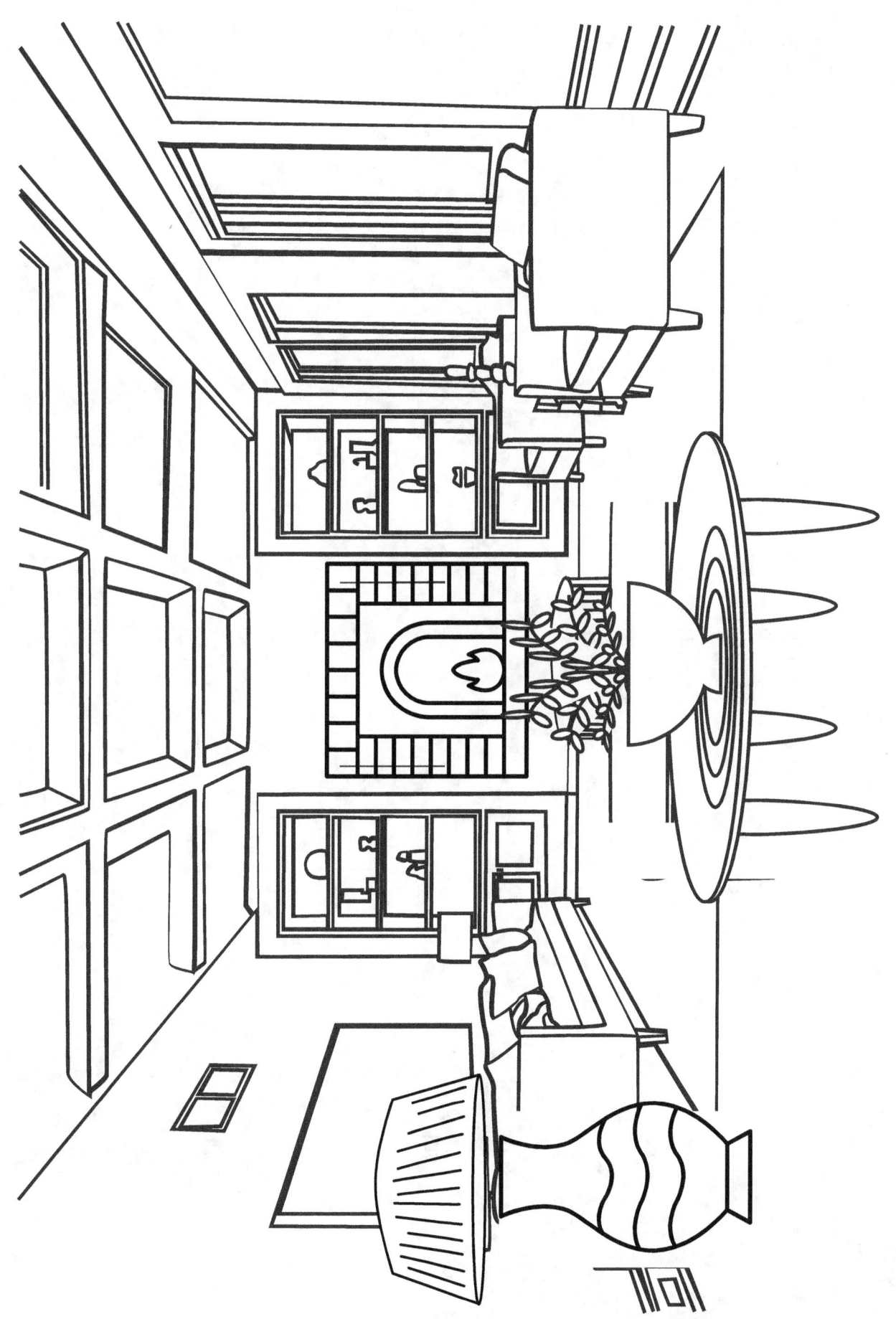

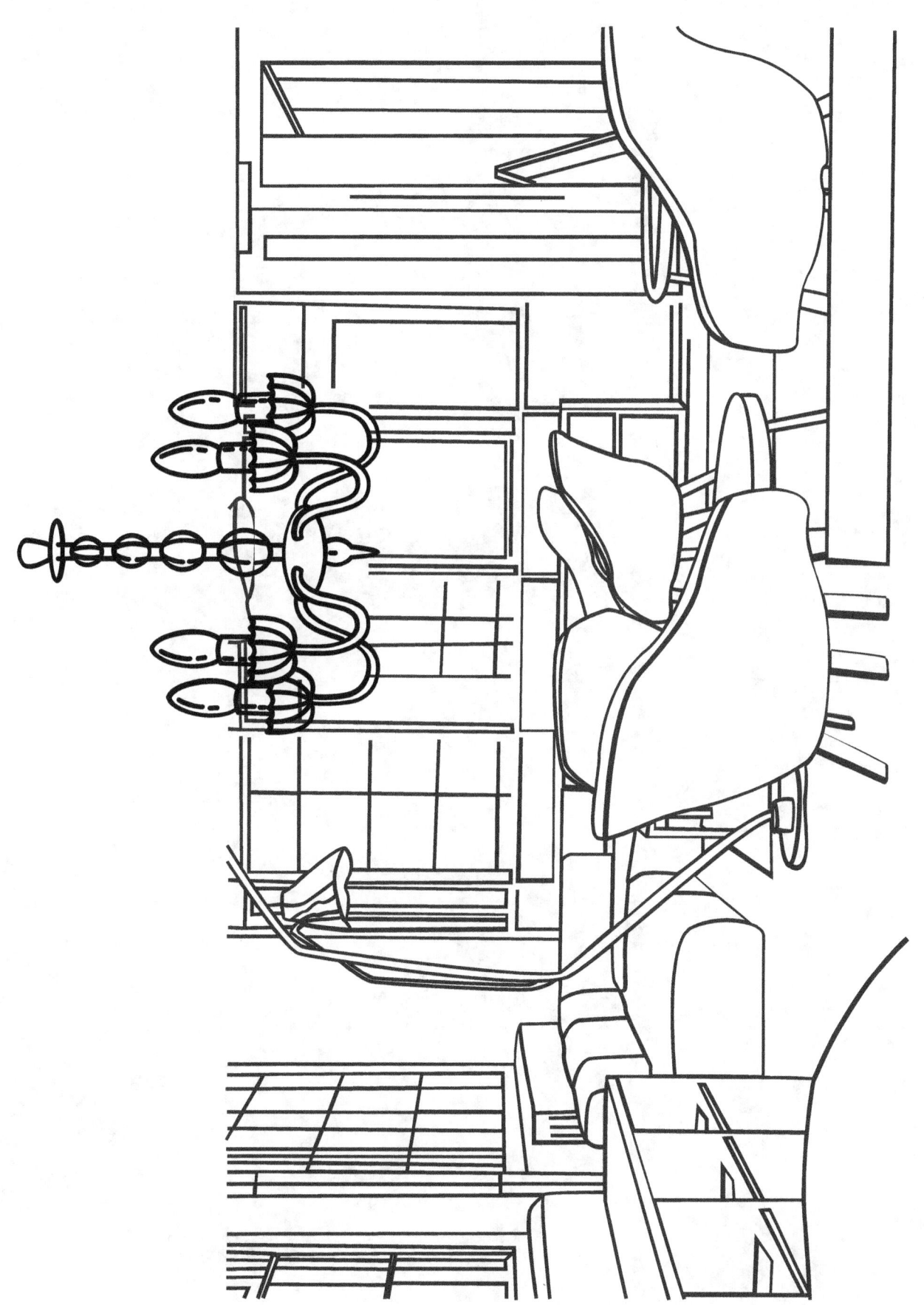

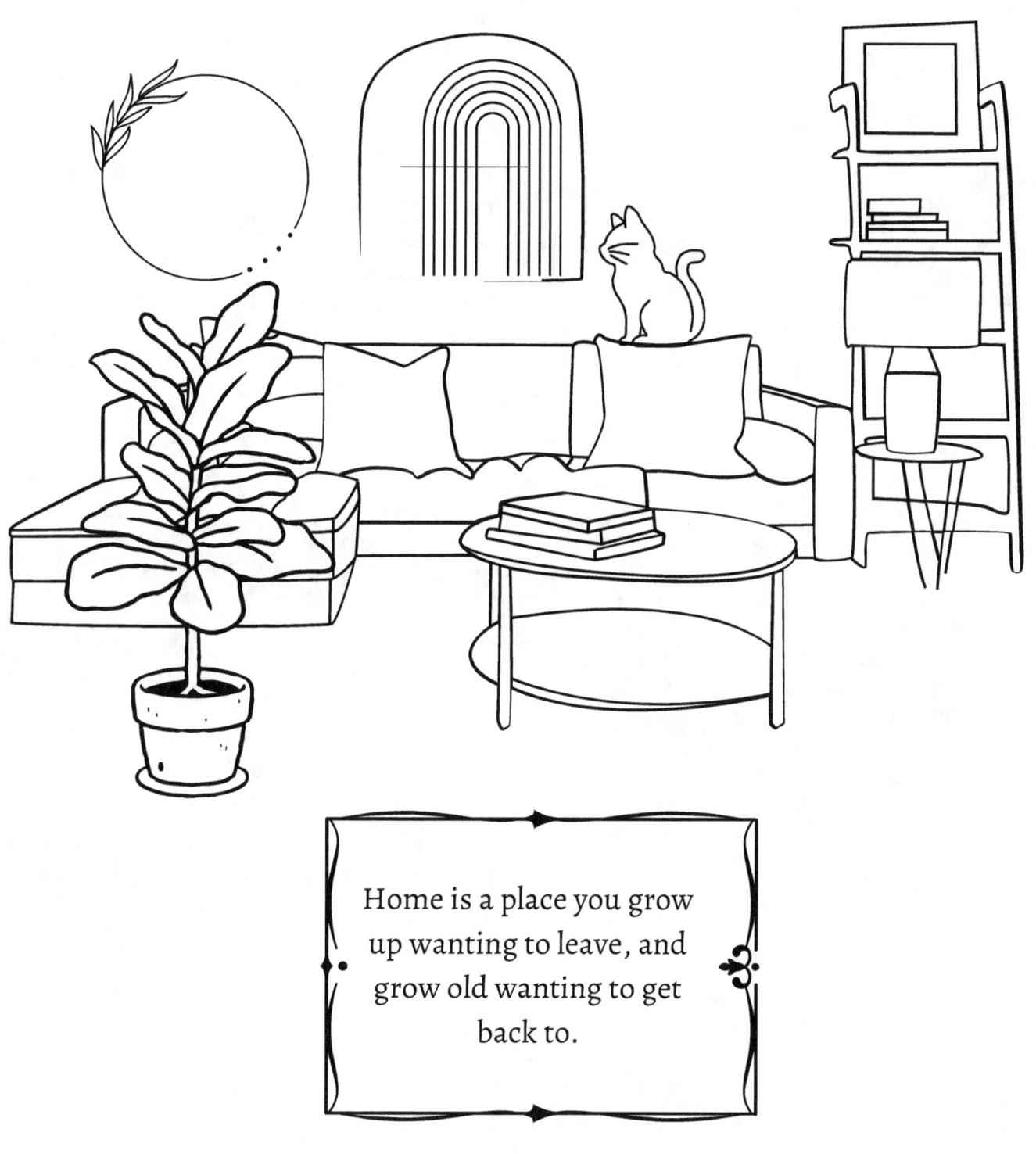

Home is a place you grow up wanting to leave, and grow old wanting to get back to.

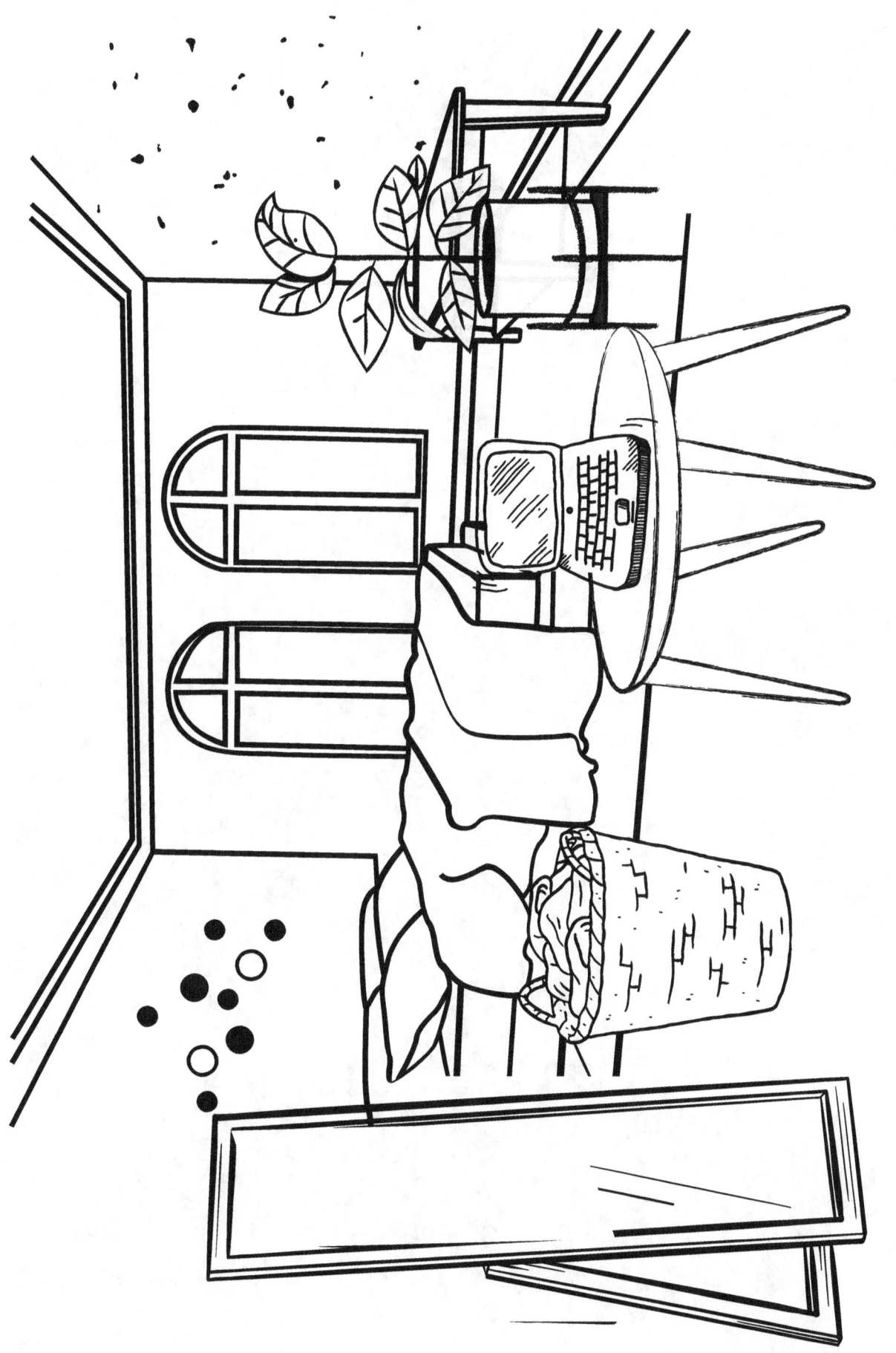

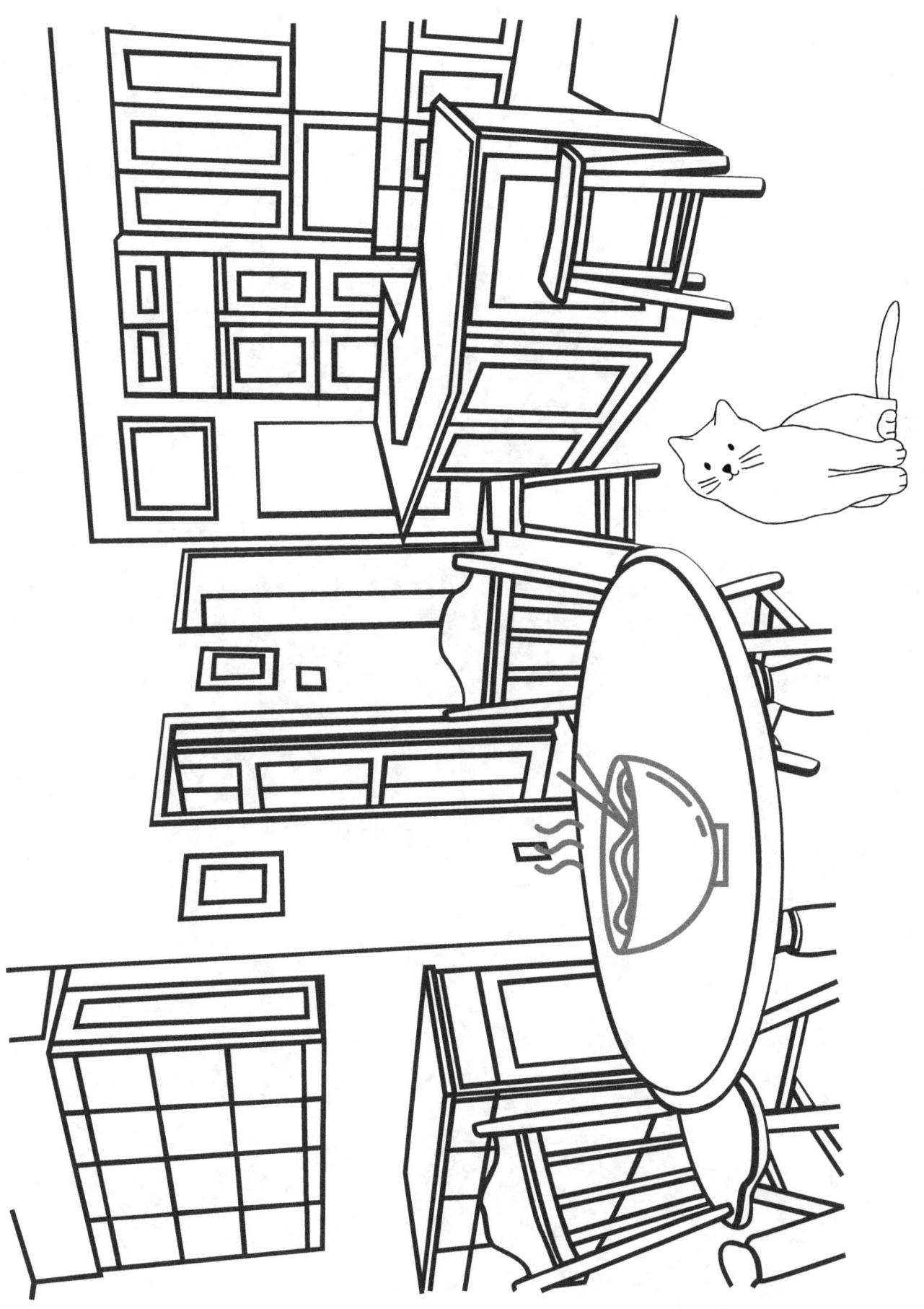

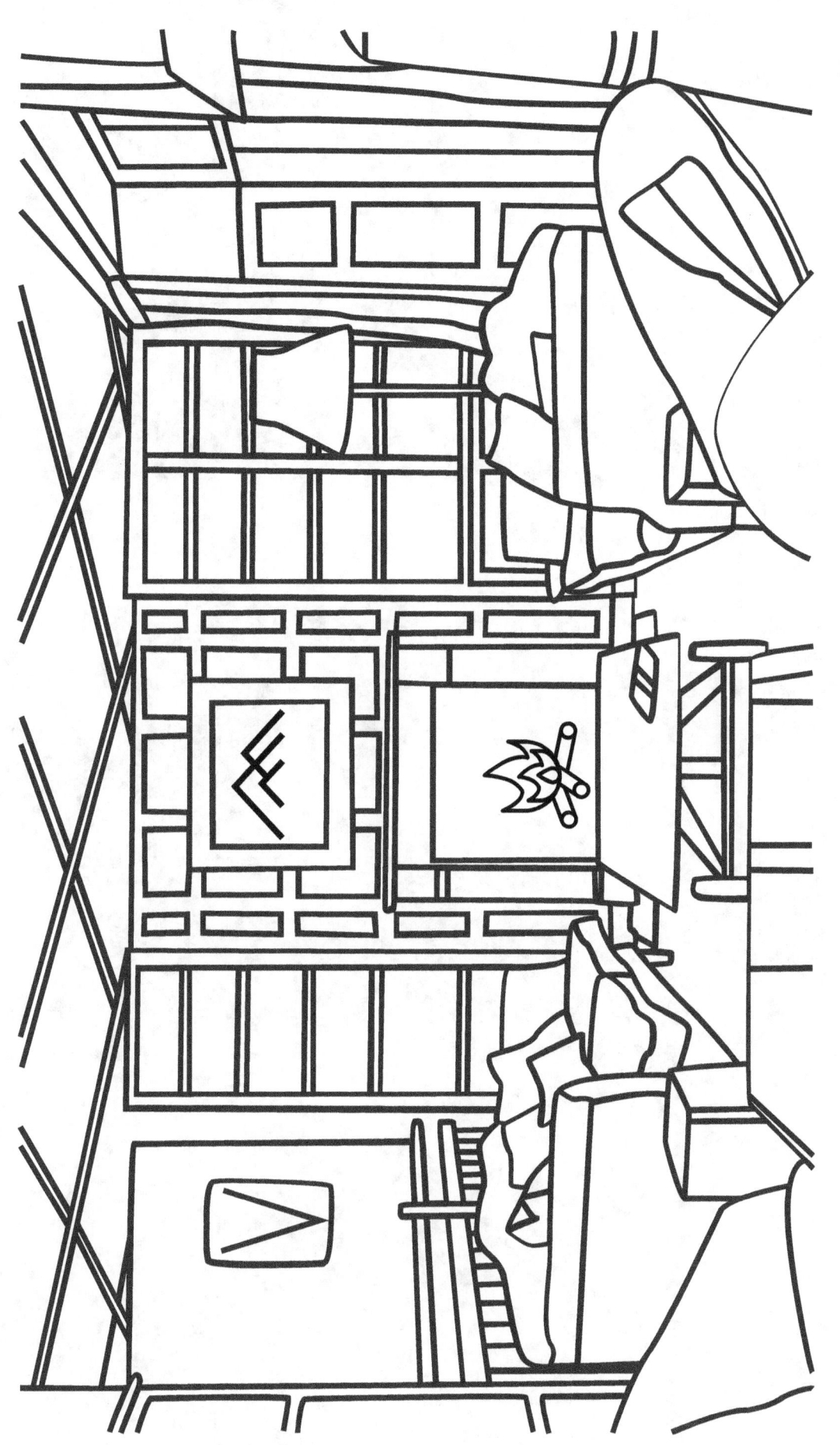

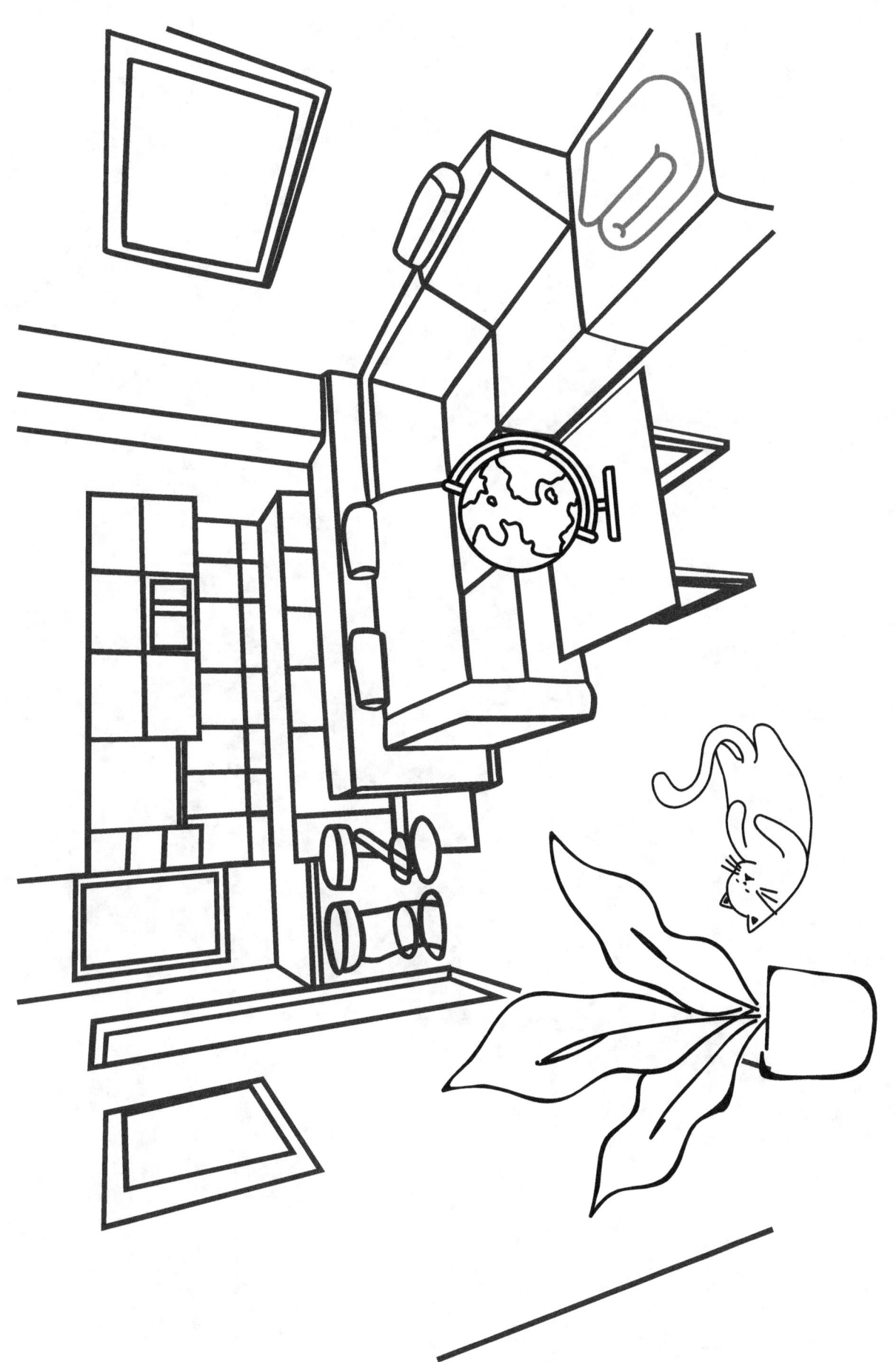

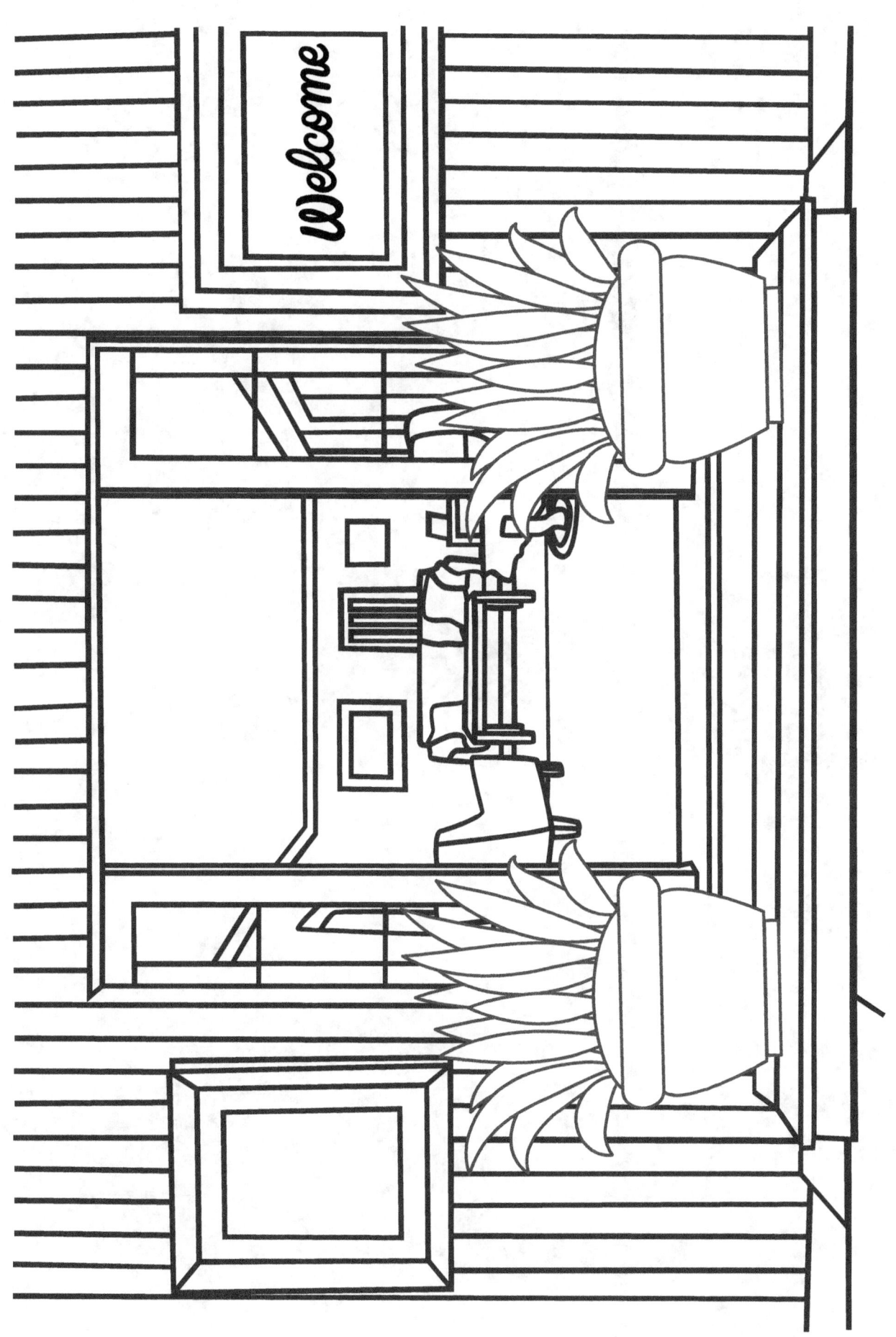

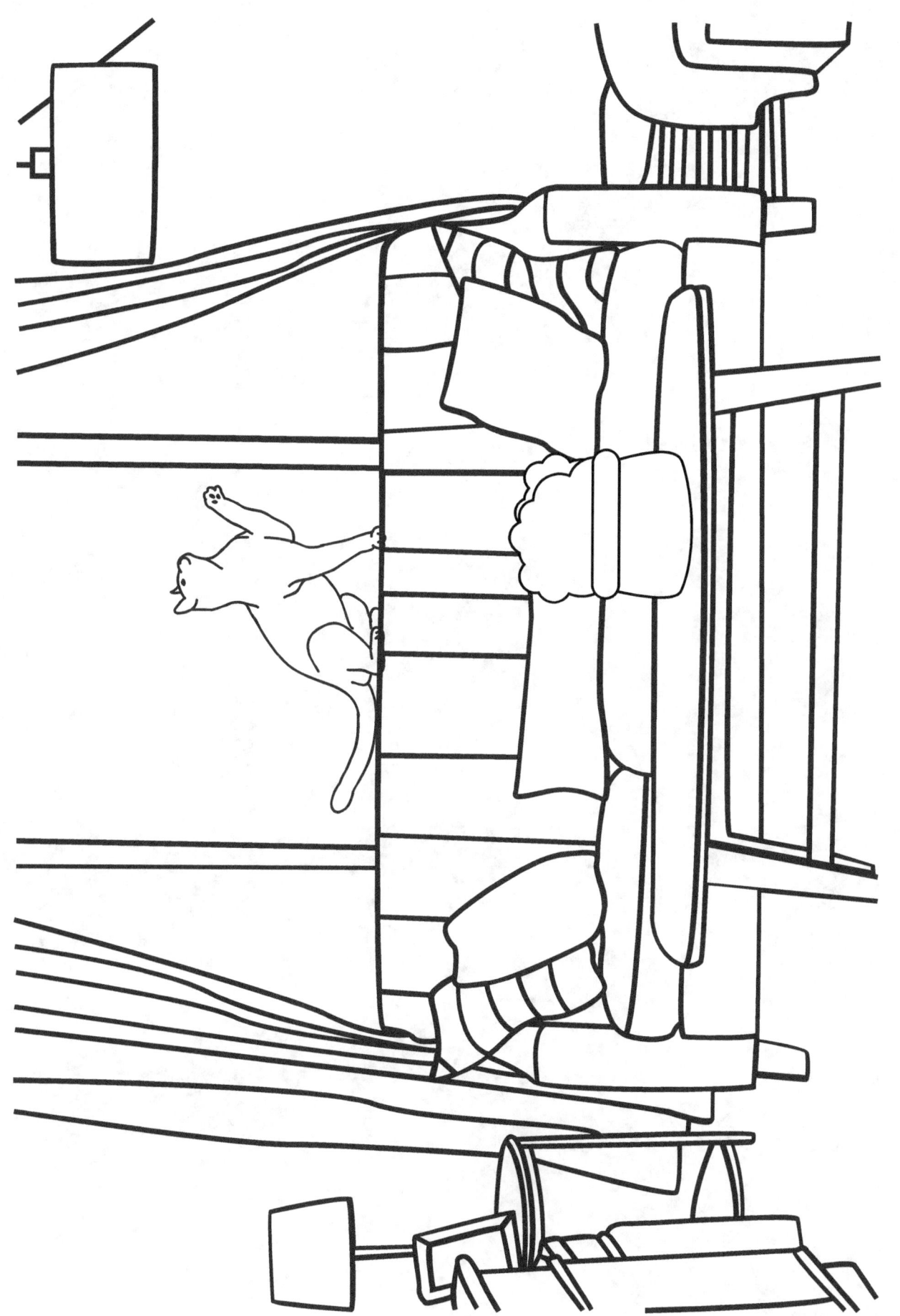

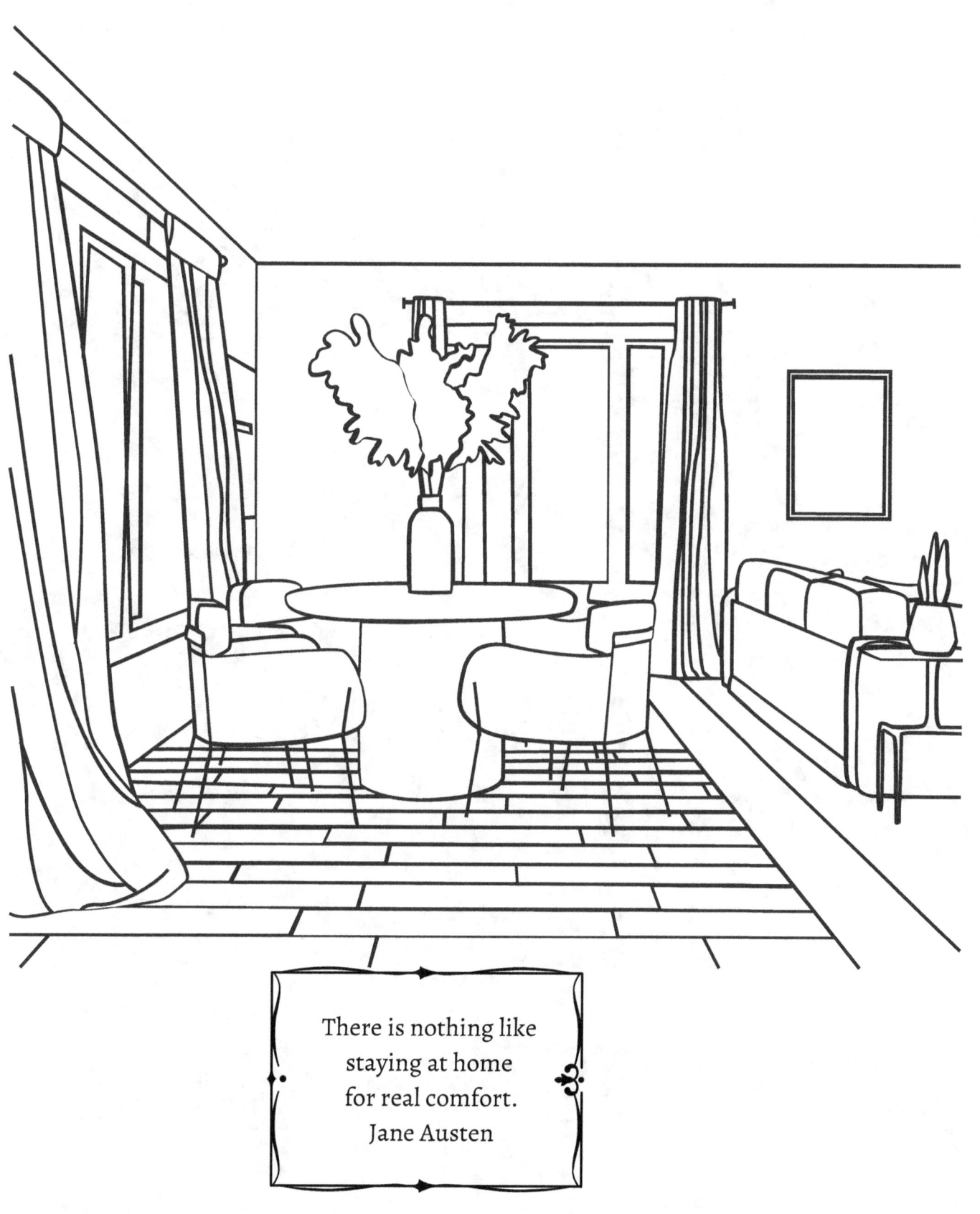

There is nothing like staying at home for real comfort.
Jane Austen

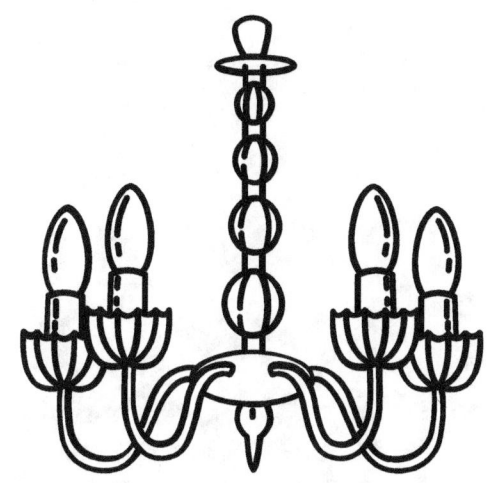

Thank you for choosing my book!
I hope you enjoyed coloring it as
much as I enjoyed making it.

Please look for my other books on Amazon~
Ms. Josephine's Papers

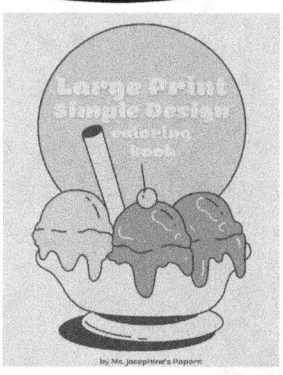
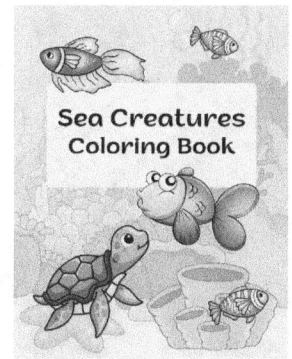
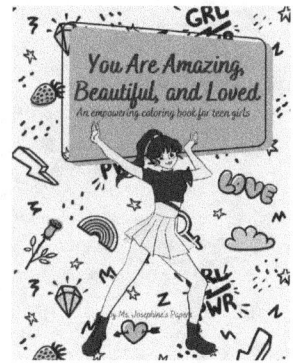
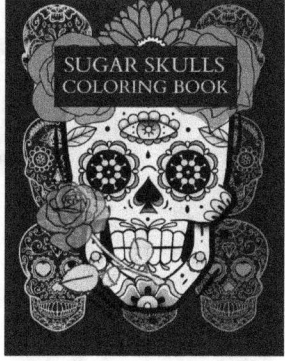
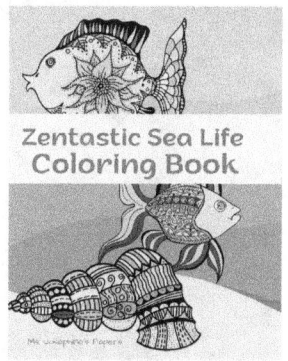

www.ingramcontent.com/pod-product-compliance
Lightning Source LLC
Chambersburg PA
CBHW080939220526
45465CB00008BA/3095